A LEGACY OF POSITIVE CONSEQUENCE

Trivers

ORO EDITIONS

Contents

Foreword

COLLABORATION AND CONSEQUENCE

BY JOHN BERGLUND

I first became aware of Trivers after meeting its founder, Andy Trivers, more than twenty-five years ago. Andy has always possessed a generous smile, warm and inviting. He has conviction, which comes from a belief that he can help and make a difference. Those qualities enabled him to establish a firm that has created architecture of lasting positive consequence for the St. Louis community and beyond for five decades and counting.

Just one year after meeting Andy, I started working at Trivers. The company was based on the 18th floor along Broadway in downtown St. Louis. The office had a fantastic view of the city, including iconic landmarks like the Gateway Arch and Old Courthouse (Trivers would eventually work on significant projects for both).

During my time at Trivers, I collaborated with experienced designers and developers on a wide variety of projects throughout St. Louis. The firm designed the renovation and addition to Adams Elementary School, a public school in a once distressed neighborhood; renovated the historic and long vacant Continental Life Building in Grand Center; reimagined a turn-of-the-century warehouse complex into the Westin Hotel downtown; and completed several affordable housing projects in partnership with McCormack Baron Salazar, including Carr Square. It impressed me that Trivers always knew how to consistently uncover quality good design, even in the most demanding environments.

My experience at Trivers taught me how to achieve successful projects on tight budgets. After ten years, including a stint at another firm, I decided to leave the architecture profession and go into business with Jim McKelvey, co-founder of Square (now known as Block). This put me on the developer side of the table, but with a unique perspective on what it took to deliver the product that Trivers was so versed in providing.

In 2018, the Post-Dispatch Building in downtown St. Louis was for sale. Constructed as part of a row of historic newspaper buildings, including The St. Louis Globe-Democrat and St. Louis Star-Times. With the last newspaper printed there in 2007, the structure was created for another time and place. However, it had great bones and history worth preserving. With the goal of repositioning the building as prime office space for St. Louis's burgeoning geospatial and financial technology ecosystem, I knew which firm to call. With decades of adaptive reuse experience, Trivers understood the lift that would be required to give new life to a structure from a bygone era.

Over the years I had stayed in touch with Joe Brinkmann, my colleague who began working at Trivers close to the same time as I did. It is a bit serendipitous that Joe started at the firm's twenty-five-year mark and stayed on for the next twenty-five. Alongside principals Amy Gilbertson and Joel Fuoss, they have led a group that has been able to continue Andy's legacy of diverse and meaningful project types.

I appreciated the insight and collaboration Trivers provided throughout the renovation of the Post-Dispatch Building. As a former architect working as a developer, I realized I had to lead with my wallet instead of my heart—and I am sure there were times when the Trivers team wished I would stay in my lane. Ultimately, we struck a good balance at what is now known as the Post Building. I am grateful for this team rooted in making a difference to help us get there.

St. Louis has such a rich history. The Post Building is just one example of the abundant opportunities for firms like Trivers to be part of the city's reinvention. Not only does Trivers welcome challenging projects, but they also have the skills and knowledge their clients need to achieve their vision.

With unforgiving market pressures of budgets and deadlines, good design can be hard to find. Undertaking a complex adaptive reuse project can add additional challenges in an already tough sector. But these limitations are important. Time and again, Trivers has proven that the best designs are born from creativity and conflict resolution as opposed to having an unlimited amount of money and time.

I periodically get asked what can be done to renew the vitality of downtown St. Louis, a city shaped by a complex history and years of disinvestment. I believe downtown St. Louis's path forward is a collaborative one where architects, developers, and the public collectively create safe environments where people want to spend their time and invest their resources. Trivers's projects, including the Post Building, embody the creativity and foresight essential in creating momentum toward meaningful and positive growth.

Fifty years is a significant milestone for one company that has made such a significant impact in areas that have needed it most. I applaud Trivers for not only surviving but continuing to flourish.

Introduction

BY JOE BRINKMANN, AIA
JOEL FUOSS, AIA
AND AMY GILBERTSON, FAIA

Trivers's fifty-year monograph is a celebration of five decades of design excellence and meaningful impact. This book chronicles the evolution of a firm shaped by a commitment to solving complex challenges, advancing sustainability, and enriching the communities we serve.

Since its founding, Trivers has been defined by its dedication to bold ideas and collaborative leadership. Our work spans adaptive reuse, preservation, and innovative new designs—all rooted in the belief that architecture has the power to inspire change. Through challenging projects and a steadfast focus on sustainability, we have sought to leave a lasting and positive legacy.

At the heart of Trivers is a culture that values collaboration, curiosity, and the collective effort of a talented team. This spirit has not only guided the firm's trajectory but also fostered strong partnerships with clients and communities alike. These shared values have enabled us to create spaces that honor their context, elevate human experiences, and respond to the needs of the present while looking toward the future.

In the pages ahead, you will find a thoughtful reflection on our journey, from defining partnerships and transformative projects to the principles that continue to shape our practice. We invite you to explore the stories, ideas, and collaborations that have defined Trivers' past and inspire our future.

nichiha.com
Prodema
LAP SIDING

Our Founder

THE LEGACY OF HISTORIC PRESERVATION PIONEER, ANDY TRIVERS, FAIA

Preservation is best achieved when buildings are not considered remnants of the past but transformed into contributing structures for contemporary society. No one understood this better than Trivers founder Andrew (Andy) Trivers, FAIA.

Originally from Chattanooga, Tennessee, Andy came to St. Louis in 1970 following graduation from architecture school at Tulane University in New Orleans to complete his master's degree in architecture at Washington University in St. Louis. He decided to stay and dedicate his career to historic preservation and adaptive reuse by starting SRT Architects and Planners with partners Pat Spector and Don Royce in 1975.

In 1983, Andy assumed full ownership of SRT Architects and Planners and renamed the firm Trivers Associates. He became one of the pioneer architects who recognized that the future success of older cities would, in part, rely on saving their architectural past. At a time when urban populations were moving to the suburbs, he remained committed to the idea that each city's unique character is defined by its historic architecture.

Andy's approach to preservation was to combine a talent for design with a clear understanding of what is important to maintain and what could be altered and improved without compromising historic integrity. He believed historic preservation is best served by careful integration of new technologies into historic buildings, making them useful members of society. When achieved, a fully functioning historic building that retains its character, memory, and detail will ensure preservation for generations into the future.

Andy's well-known expertise in the field of historic preservation provided him the opportunity to work on exceptional buildings and sites in dozens of other states. These include the US Custom House and Old Post Office in St. Louis, Missouri; the US Post Office & Courthouse in New Bern, North Carolina; Hipolito F. Garcia Federal Building and US Courthouse in San Antonio, Texas; Tobacco Row in Richmond, Virginia; and Canal Square in Akron, Ohio.

His work on multiple typologies—including civic, education, housing, cultural, and hospitality—earned more than thirty international, national, state and local awards. The American Institute of Architects (AIA) recognized him with six awards and elevated him to its prestigious College of Fellows in 2011. He also was honored with Washington University's Sam Fox School of Design & Visual Arts Distinguished Alumnus in Architecture Award in 2005. Three years later, he proudly accepted the Initiative for a Competitive Inner City's Inner City 100 Award on behalf of Trivers, which was ranked as one of the top 100 fastest growing inner-city companies in America out of a pool of more than 12,000 nominees.

Over the course of forty years, Andy shaped Trivers into a nationally recognized leader in historic preservation and adaptive reuse. Under his leadership, the firm grew from three to fifty individuals. In 2015, he transitioned ownership to a new leadership group that shared the core principles upon which he founded the company in 1975.

> From the start, I was impressed with the grand heritage of St. Louis architecture. I developed a sensitivity to historic structures and recognized the need for cities to retain their individual identities through adaptive reuse and historic preservation.

ANDY TRIVERS, ST. LOUIS COMMERCE MAGAZINE, 1988

WASHINGTON APARTMENTS RIBBON CUTTING, 1980
ANDY TRIVERS PICTURED FAR RIGHT

Enduring Partnerships

Trivers is profoundly grateful for all the partners it has collaborated with to build a legacy of positive consequence over the last fifty years. Long-lasting relationships with McCormack Baron Salazar, Washington University, American Cancer Society, the United States General Services Administration, and Grice Group Architects have not only vastly contributed to Trivers's success but also resulted in dozens of projects that strengthen communities and enhance the built environment.

McCormack Baron Salazar

1976 - PRESENT

AKRON, OH
CINCINNATI, OH
CLEVELAND, OH
JERSEY CITY, NJ
KANSAS CITY, MO
LOUISVILLE, KY
PITTSBURGH, PA
RICHMOND, VA
SAINT LOUIS, MO
SPRINGFIELD, IL

Trivers's founder, Andy Trivers, envisioned transforming the historic George Washington Hotel in St. Louis's Central West End neighborhood into the Washington Apartments. All he needed was a development partner, and his meeting with Richard Baron, co-founder and chairman of McCormack Baron Salazar (MBS), proved pivotal. It not only resulted in Trivers's first project but also laid the foundation for both firms' legacies of creating architecture with lasting impact.

The seven-story, 89,000-square-foot George Washington Hotel was originally built in 1903 for the 1904 World's Fair but had been vacant for many years. Andy and Richard revitalized the building by turning it into affordable housing while preserving its grandeur.

The project catalyzed a decades-long partnership between Trivers and MBS. Over the years, the firms have collaborated on dozens of adaptive reuse projects that have resulted in more than 3,500 affordable housing units. One of their most groundbreaking projects, 6 North Apartments in the Central West End, was the first large-scale, multi-family rental development in the United States to feature Universal Design in all units. Beyond St. Louis, Tobacco Row in Richmond, Virginia, one of the state's largest historic tax credit projects, reconnected downtown Richmond to the James River and established a new residential and urban neighborhood.

Trivers and MBS recognized that, in addition to housing, other project types can also make a lasting and meaningful impact. The adaptive reuse of the historic Woolworth Building in St. Louis's Midtown neighborhood provided a home for community-focused organizations, including Big Brothers Big Sisters of Eastern Missouri and the Kranzberg Arts Center. Built in one of Missouri's lowest-income ZIP codes, the I. Jerome and Rosemary Flance Early Learning Center provides critical resources as both an early childhood education center and a community health care center. In 2001, MBS and Trivers partnered on one of St. Louis's largest redevelopment projects, transforming four deteriorating warehouses into the Westin and spurring the renewal of the Cupples Station Historic District. In addition to housing and community-focused projects, Trivers collaborated with MBS on the design of their corporate offices—first in 2010 and again in 2022—further solidifying a longstanding partnership built on shared values.

Washington
Washington
WASHINGTON
APARTMENTS

From our first project together to the many that followed, we've held a shared belief that our work strengthens communities and improves people's lives. Over the years, our collaboration on thoughtful planning and design has transformed underinvested structures and neighborhoods into places that once again foster opportunity. Much of the MBS mission has been manifested into the built reality through our partnership with Trivers to bring this important work to life.

RICHARD BARON
CHAIRMAN, MCCORMACK BARON SALAZAR

PREVIOUS PAGE Washington Apartments

LEFT Brewery Apartments

RIGHT TOP MBS Corporate Headquarters

RIGHT BOTTOM Allen Market Lane Apartments

NEXT PAGE Woolworth Building

BIG BROTHERS BIG SISTERS
BIG BROTHERS

BIG SISTER
KRANZBERG

Washington University in St. Louis

1990 - PRESENT

DANFORTH CAMPUS
MEDICAL CAMPUS
NORTH CAMPUS
WEST CAMPUS

The Danforth Campus of Washington University in St. Louis (WashU), a National Historic Landmark, is one of four campuses where Trivers has proudly contributed to preserving the university's legacy while ensuring its continued functionality for modern needs. With many Trivers team members being WashU alumni, the firm's connection to the university extends beyond projects to a shared investment in its legacy. For more than three decades, Trivers has collaborated with WashU on more than sixty historic preservation and new construction projects, allowing its structures to remain cultural resources and touchstones for the city.

Trivers's relationship with WashU began following the passage of the Americans with Disabilities Act (ADA) in 1990. Recognizing Trivers's expertise in historic preservation, WashU engaged the firm to conduct an accessibility analysis of the Danforth Campus. The completion of the analysis and efforts to bring several structures into ADA compliance led WashU to select Trivers for the 2006 renovation of Wilson Hall. The project included a two-story atrium, new faculty offices, an elevator, and significant upgrades to the auditorium.

On the heels of the successful transformation of Wilson Hall, Trivers worked with WashU on several other major projects, including Umrath Hall, one of the most important historic structures on campus. Originally constructed as a dormitory, Trivers designed an entirely new building within the original façade. By removing the roof and demolishing the second floor and bearing walls, Trivers increased low floor-to-floor heights and created flexible classroom and academic spaces.

WashU has also turned to Trivers to help make campus operations truly sustainable. One iconic building that fell below the university's sustainability standards was January Hall, which was constructed in 1922 to house the School of Law. Trivers upgraded the façade with new windows, insulation, roofing, mechanical systems, and low-flow plumbing, while also transforming an outdated lecture hall into a modern, flexible learning space and renovating the East Asian Library. The project exceeded the university's sustainability goals by achieving LEED Platinum certification.

Trivers's collaboration with WashU established a strong foundation for the firm's growing education practice, leading to work with colleges and universities nationwide that honor campus architectural legacies while fostering exceptional learning environments.

WASHINGTON UNIVERSITY

Trivers' institutional knowledge and understanding of our campus planning goals, design excellence aspirations and raising the bar on sustainability is truly admirable. We look forward to many more years of fostering the symbiotic relationship that we have developed with them.

ED SOLTERO, PH.D., FAIA, LEED AP BD+C
ASSISTANT VICE-CHANCELLOR AND UNIVERSITY ARCHITECT, WASHINGTON UNIVERSITY

PREVIOUS PAGE January Hall

LEFT Bryan Hall (Associate Architect to Ayers Saint Gross)

RIGHT TOP Umrath Hall

RIGHT BOTTOM Ann Whitney Olin Women's Building

NEXT PAGE Wilson Hall

American Cancer Society

1992 - PRESENT

BIRMINGHAM, AL
JACKSON, MS
KANSAS CITY, MO
LEXINGTON, KY
LUBBOCK, TX
MEMPHIS, TN
NASHVILLE, TN
NEW ORLEANS, LA
OMAHA, NE
PHILADELPHIA, PA
SAINT LOUIS, MO

–

The American Cancer Society (ACS) and Trivers have collaborated for decades to design dozens of Hope Lodge communities, which serve as homes away from home for cancer patients and their caregivers who must travel for treatment.

Before the Hope Lodge program, many cancer patients reported sleeping in their vehicles, driving long distances to and from home, or avoiding treatment altogether due to the cost of lodging. Today, Hope Lodge communities provide more than just a free place to stay—they offer nurturing, homelike environments where patients can access the care they need.

The first Hope Lodge designed by Trivers was among the first in the United States. Completed in 1995, the ACS Hope Lodge in St. Louis served as a model for future projects nationwide, many of which Trivers led. In 2015, Trivers helped ACS introduce a new design model for Hope Lodge communities, incorporating features known to improve health outcomes. The updated lodge program includes guest suites with separate living and sleeping areas, open kitchens with island seating that foster shared connection, and outdoor amenities such as landscaped walking paths and seating areas. Interior biophilic design elements further enhance the connection to nature.

This model recognizes that cancer patients' treatments and experiences are as personal and unique as they are. Over the past decade, Trivers has served as lead architect for the renovation of the St. Louis Hope Lodge, as well as new facilities in Omaha, Nebraska, and Jackson, Mississippi. Additionally, Trivers is designing renovations to align existing Hope Lodges with the new model in Kentucky, Missouri, Tennessee, and Texas.

Trivers is proud to support ACS in its mission to ease the journeys of cancer patients and their caregivers through design that promotes comfort, reflection, and rejuvenation. Currently, the thirty-two American Cancer Society Hope Lodge locations nationwide collectively provide 500,000 nights of free lodging annually, saving 29,000 cancer patients and caregivers more than $55 million in lodging costs each year.

American Cancer Society
World Wide Technology
Hope Lodge
4207
SPEED LIMIT 5
OUR CITY. OUR SCHOOLS. OUR FUTURE.

The Hope Lodge program has a tremendous positive impact on patients and their caregivers. Trivers consistently provides design solutions that support bettering health outcomes and an improved experience in what can be a difficult journey.

WILLIAM ETHIER SR.
DIRECTOR, CONSTRUCTION MANAGEMENT, AMERICAN CANCER SOCIETY

PREVIOUS PAGE Hope Lodge, Jackson, MS

LEFT Hope Lodge, St. Louis, MO

TOP RIGHT Hope Lodge, Omaha, NE

BOTTOM RIGHT Hope Lodge, St. Louis, MO

NEXT PAGE Hope Lodge, Omaha, NE

General Services Administration

1994 - PRESENT

BOSTON, MA
CAPE GIRARDEAU, MO
INDIANAPOLIS, IN
MONTPELIER, VT
NEW BERN, NC
NEW HAVEN, CT
PROVIDENCE, RI
SAINT LOUIS, MO
SALT LAKE CITY, UT
SAN ANTONIO, TX

–

Trivers's longstanding partnership with the United States General Services Administration (GSA) reflects a shared commitment to creating enduring legacies for significant public spaces.

GSA helps federal agencies build and acquire office space, products, and other workplace services while overseeing the preservation of historic federal properties. After completing several renovations for GSA-owned buildings—including the Old Post Office in St. Louis, then considered the sixth most significant structure in GSA's inventory—Trivers won its first GSA Design Excellence Program project: revitalizing the Hipolito F. Garcia Federal Building and US Courthouse. Upon completion in 2012, the project earned LEED Platinum certification from the US Green Building Council—a first for a GSA-owned historic building.

The successful renovation of the Garcia Federal Building led GSA to select Trivers for several additional high-profile projects, as well as support roles within GSA's historic building portfolio. Completed in 2024, Trivers led design efforts for the $46 million renovation and the creation of new workspaces for multiple federal agencies within the Major General Emmett J. Bean Federal Center in Indianapolis—one of the country's largest military facilities, second only to the Pentagon. Trivers also serves as the lead historic architect, in partnership with lead architect HOK, on the $120 million seismic upgrade, backfill, and renovation of the Frank E. Moss U.S. Courthouse in Salt Lake City. A milestone for GSA, this project is the agency's first seismic retrofit within a historic building to receive a "No Adverse Effect" designation.

GSA has recognized Trivers as a thought leader in rehabilitating historic structures. Andy Trivers, the firm's founder, is featured in *Voices of Sustainable Building*, Vision + Voice Volume 4, a publication documenting the history of the GSA Design Excellence Program. Additionally, Trivers Principal Amy Gilbertson serves on GSA's National Registry of Peer Professionals, a network of industry leaders who provide guidance at critical milestones for GSA capital projects.

Trivers's ability to implement modern improvements for accessibility, security, and operational excellence—while respecting a building's history and context—continues to complement GSA's mission: "creating financially and environmentally sustainable, accessible, and responsive workplace solutions that enable a productive federal workforce."

STATES OF AMERICA

UNITED STATES OF AMERICA

Trivers always has the best interest of the significant materials and spaces in mind, while acknowledging the need for sympathetic modern interventions to keep the buildings viable.

GSA REGIONAL HISTORIC PRESERVATION OFFICER

PREVIOUS PAGE Frank E. Moss US Courthouse, Salt Lake City, UT

LEFT US Post Office and Courthouse, New Bern, NC

RIGHT Hipolito F. Garcia Federal Building and US Courthouse, San Antonio, TX

NEXT PAGE Major General Emmett J. Bean Federal Center, Indianapolis, IN

111 F
111 F

Grice Group Architects

1994 - PRESENT

For over three decades, Trivers and Grice Group Architects have combined their expertise on projects that serve housing, education, cultural, and community-focused clients. Their long-standing collaboration culminated in the formation of Grice-Trivers Joint Venture Architects in 2010, further enhancing both firms' capacity to serve shared clients and mobilize resources for larger-scale initiatives.

Grice Group Architects, founded in 1984 by Karl A. Grice, FAIA, brings decades of architectural and planning experience, with a strong commitment to serving diverse communities. As a Minority Business Enterprise (MBE), Grice Group is the majority holder of the Joint Venture, ensuring a collaborative approach that amplifies both firms' strengths.

Together, the Joint Venture has delivered a wide range of impactful projects across the region-from affordable housing developments such as Adams Grove Housing and St. Louis Housing Authority initiatives, to major educational and institutional endeavors including work at Lambert St. Louis International Airport, St. Louis Public School District and Harris-Stowe State University. Through this dynamic collaboration, the firms continue to play a pivotal role in shaping St. Louis's built environment while steadily broadening their regional impact.

4472 A

Our partnership with Trivers over the last thirty-plus years has always been about collaboration and a shared commitment to serving communities. Through the joint venture, we have been able to deliver transformative projects that have made a lasting impact on the region by expanding housing, educational and cultural opportunities.

KARL GRICE, FAIA
PRINCIPAL, GRICE GROUP ARCHITECTS

PREVIOUS PAGE Adams Grove

LEFT Harris-Stowe State University Bosley Hall

RIGHT TOP Compton Hill Water Tower

RIGHT BOTTOM St. Louis Housing Authority Office Building

NEXT PAGE Adams Grove

ADT

4437 B
4437 A

Projects

Across five decades, Trivers has embraced the belief that buildings can inspire meaningful change. The projects featured here reflect our commitment to addressing complex challenges with thoughtful design, advancing sustainable practices, and creating lasting community impact. Together, they illustrate how architecture can be a catalyst for change while shaping a more intentional and equitable future.

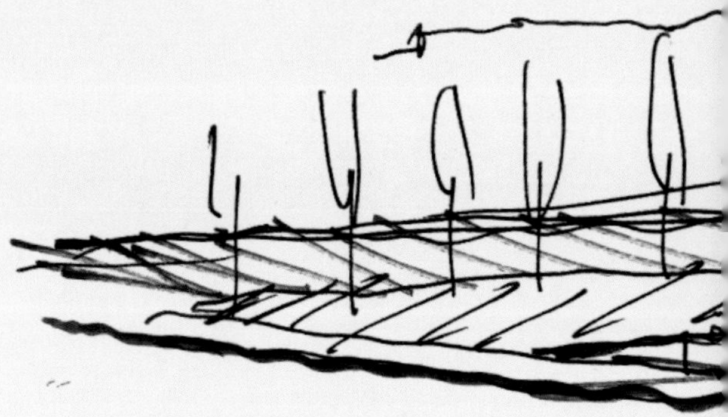

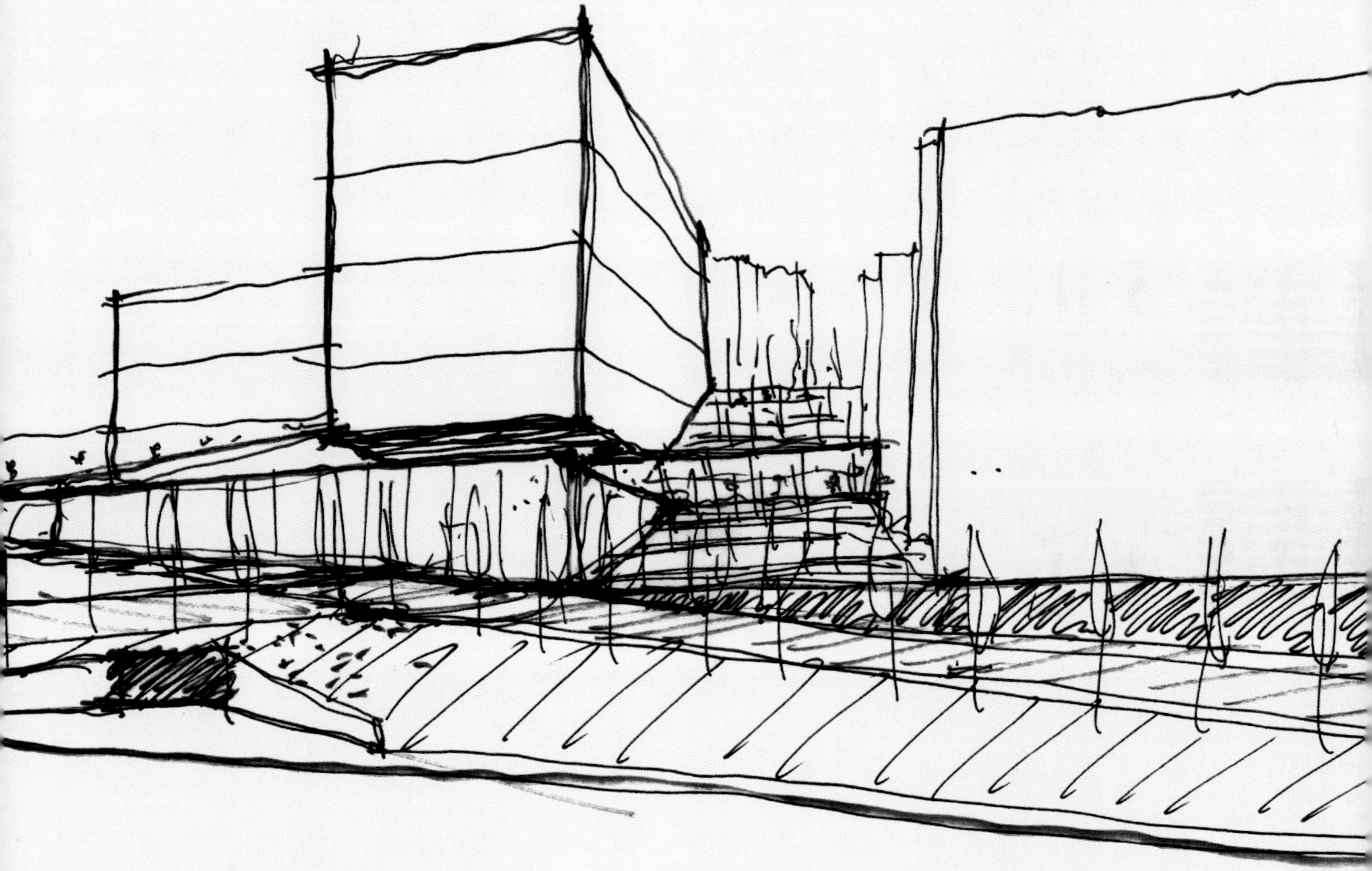

THE WES

2001 The Westin

LOCATION
SAINT LOUIS, MO
DOWNTOWN

TYPE
HOSPITALITY

CLIENT
MCCORMACK
BARON SALAZAR

The Cupples Station Historic District in downtown St. Louis once consisted of ten late 19th-century warehouses built to house goods destined for shipment west of the Mississippi River to the burgeoning western United States. Developer McCormack Baron Salazar engaged Trivers to breathe new life into four of these historic structures, transforming them into a 21st-century hotel.

The design solution needed to strike a balance between preserving the historic architectural character of the existing warehouse buildings and meeting the programmatic requirements of a four-star hotel. The team proceeded to rehabilitate the neglected structures in a way that would unify the four buildings while serving the needs of modern travelers in a setting deeply rooted in St. Louis's history.

The entire project was organized around the entry courtyard, which had formerly served as a truck loading dock. Transforming the heart of the former warehouse system into the central arrival point of the hotel, the guest experience now echoes the historic movement of goods—only now, it is people arriving rather than merchandise. A distinctly modern glass-and-steel bridge connecting all four buildings, along with glass canopies, provides a contemporary counterpoint to the historic setting while emphasizing the landscaped central court.

The exterior renovation included a complete restoration of each building's masonry, the installation of seismic bracing, and the replacement of every window and door in accordance with the Secretary of the Interior's

Trivers made absolutely the most of the existing architectural detail of the building, then further enhanced it with a courtyard to tie the fourth, unconnected (although it will be, by elevated walkways) building in the complex to the other three.

***RIVERFRONT TIMES*, BEST OF ST. LOUIS 2000**

Standards for Rehabilitation. Additionally, extensive public improvements—including new sidewalks, street trees, and lighting—enhanced the outward approach to the hotel's chosen flag, the Westin, the first of its brand in the St. Louis market.

At the building owner's request, the Westin's interior was distinctly modern, featuring natural materials that harmonize with the building's existing architecture while deliberately contrasting with its historic shell. Exposed concrete columns and brickwork are juxtaposed with undulating wood walls highlighted by dramatic lighting in the hotel's public spaces and guest rooms. Nestled within the buildings, hotel patrons enjoy meeting rooms, a ballroom, executive lounge, and a full-service restaurant, also open to the public. The hotel's 255 guest rooms feature artwork by local artists, reinforcing the design team's goal of creating a unique St. Louis experience.

The Westin's opening in 2001 and its ongoing success catalyzed the revitalization of the remaining historic buildings in the district, setting a precedent for their preservation and reuse. The historic architecture of Cupples Station served as the design inspiration for the St. Louis Cardinals' $500 million investment in constructing the newest Busch Stadium in 2006. The ongoing development surrounding the stadium, including the expansion of the vibrant Ballpark Village entertainment district, has brought the team's total investment in downtown St. Louis to well over $750 million since 2005.

Rather than being left as a relic of 19th-century mercantile commerce, the Westin represented a renewed investment in the city. It has since become a landmark in the revitalization of downtown St. Louis and one of the stabilizing properties that helped pave the way for the Cardinals' new stadium and its subsequent development.

LEFT Exterior Before

RIGHT Exterior After

WESTIN
WESTIN
TICKETS
pepsi
pepsi

6
NORTH
SIX NORTH
COFFEE CO.

2005 6 North Apartments

LOCATION
SAINT LOUIS, MO
CENTRAL WEST END

TYPE
MULTI-FAMILY

CLIENT
MCCORMACK
BARON SALAZAR

Situated in the Central West End neighborhood in St. Louis, 6 North Apartments stands as the country's first large-scale, multi-family development to feature comprehensive Universal Design. Universal Design promotes inclusivity, creating environments that everyone can use, with and without physical disabilities, while maintaining the look and feel of a typical apartment building.

The site of 6 North Apartments originally included an 85,700-square-foot, two-story brick warehouse constructed in 1915, along with five open-air metal canopies. In 2000, a neighboring apartment building that provided subsidized housing for residents was condemned. The building's owner, a nonprofit organization dedicated to providing independent living services for those with disabilities, worked with local leaders to help create accessible housing for the displaced residents.

Trivers was selected as the lead architect for 6 North Apartments, a development that guided the neighborhood's evolution from light industrial use to a vibrant mixed-use community featuring residential and retail spaces. Collaborating closely with the contractor, owner, community members, and Universal Design experts, Trivers delivered a building that prioritized both affordability and accessibility while adhering to Universal Design standards.

Completed in 2005, 6 North Apartments features barrier-free access. Eighty one-bedroom and two-bedroom units include adjustable cabinets with pull-out shelves, varied counter heights, drawer-style dishwashers, raised

laundry and ovens, and side-by-side refrigerators and freezers. To integrate Universal Design elements into the interiors, Trivers developed creative solutions using available products, such as a hydraulic island top that can be easily adjusted to accommodate users at different heights, whether standing or seated.

In addition to following Universal Design principles, Trivers honored the site's past by preserving the last remaining steel canopy. The canopy was repurposed as the primary organizational axis for the building's entrance, guiding residents, visitors, and customers to the main door. The building's curved corners—a common architectural feature at the time of its original construction—reflect the rounded corner of the adjacent structure across the street.

Thirty-five units are designated as affordable housing, with thirty reserved for residents earning 60 percent of the area median income (AMI) and five for those earning 50 percent AMI. Many residents benefit from Universal Design features, which improve accessibility and functionality to accommodate a range of needs.

The ingenuity and passion behind the redevelopment of 6 North Apartments were recognized regionally and nationally, earning awards such as the John M. Clancy Award for Socially Responsible Housing from the Boston Society of Architects. The building was also featured in a *New York Times* article highlighting the benefits of Universal Design and its positive impact on residents. Additionally, the project was incorporated into the twelfth edition of *The Architectural Graphic Standards* as a benchmark model for Universal Design.

The project is groundbreaking in a lot of ways, not the least of which is its universality, and has already had a catalytic effect on improving the immediate neighborhood.

JACK HAMBENE
FORMER SENIOR VICE PRESIDENT,
MCCORMACK BARON SALAZAR

2006 US Custom House and Old Post Office

LOCATION
SAINT LOUIS, MO
DOWNTOWN

TYPE
CIVIC
MIXED-USE

CLIENT
DESCO/DFC GROUP

St. Louis's US Custom House and Old Post Office (more commonly known as the Old Post Office) was built in 1872 and designated a National Historic Landmark in 1968. As part of an ongoing contract with the United States General Services Administration (GSA), Trivers was engaged to execute a variety of projects at the Old Post Office. Subsequently, the development team of DESCO and DFC Group acquired the 242,000-square-foot structure from the GSA with the intention of redeveloping it into a mixed-use commercial and institutional building in the heart of St. Louis's historic central business district.

At the time of redevelopment, the Old Post Office ranked as the sixth most important structure in GSA's inventory. Because of its significant historic status, preservation was highly prioritized, and great care was taken to avoid any unnecessary adverse impact on the building and its character-defining features. The project required close collaboration with a range of stakeholders, from state legislators and building tenants to neighboring downtown residents.

GSA and the design team defined four levels of architectural significance for all parts of the Old Post Office to appropriately allocate funds. Areas of higher historical and architectural significance received the costliest renovations.

The three most historically important spaces were restored so they could function as they did when the building was first constructed. First, the grand post office lobby on the main

level was re-established as a lobby for a future post office, a registration area for a tenant university, and access to retail. This effort included rebuilding and relocating the original wooden postal partitions, installing new, refabricated historical lighting, and restoring finishes and original brass mailboxes. Second, the Missouri Court of Appeals moved into the top two floors, reutilizing the building's primary historic courtrooms. Work in both spaces included plaster and marble restoration and the installation of historically sympathetic lighting, painting, and wooden casework restoration.

Providing programming, planning and design for multiple tenants and budgets was a primary challenge for the design team. The Missouri Court of Appeals fit seamlessly into the historic courtrooms. Webster University—with more limited financial means—chose to occupy the two lowest floors, known as the "moat level." Because of less historic scrutiny, Webster was able to build out instructional classrooms at a lower cost.

Additional interior improvements included the removal of incompatible modern interventions to uncover the building's original grandeur. Two historic restrooms with fixtures from the 1920s were restored. All ductwork and feeders were carefully concealed in existing closets and shafts. Security enhancements were seamlessly integrated into the building's original architecture, resulting in a welcoming environment that also addresses modern security concerns for public buildings.

When completed in 2006, all work met the Secretary of the Interior's Standards for Rehabilitation and was widely recognized as a success of downtown St. Louis's renaissance. Fully leased upon completion, the building served as a catalyst for more than $400 million in additional redevelopment on adjacent parcels. Restored to its original beauty and architectural integrity, the Old Post Office became a centerpiece of a once-quiet section of downtown St. Louis, poised to withstand the test of time as the city evolves around it.

With an attention to detail that did not lose sight of the big picture, Trivers provided guidance through the labyrinth of historic preservation issues. The end result is the renovation of a national monument that will withstand the test of time.

GWEN KNIGHT
FORMER VICE PRESIDENT, DEVELOPMENT AND CORPORATE SERVICES, DESCO GROUP

LEFT Restored Historic Courtroom

RIGHT Restored Historic Corridor

LEFT Restored Exterior Facade

RIGHT Central Stair and Lobby Before + After

LEFT Restored Postal Screens

RIGHT Lobby and Tenant Entrances

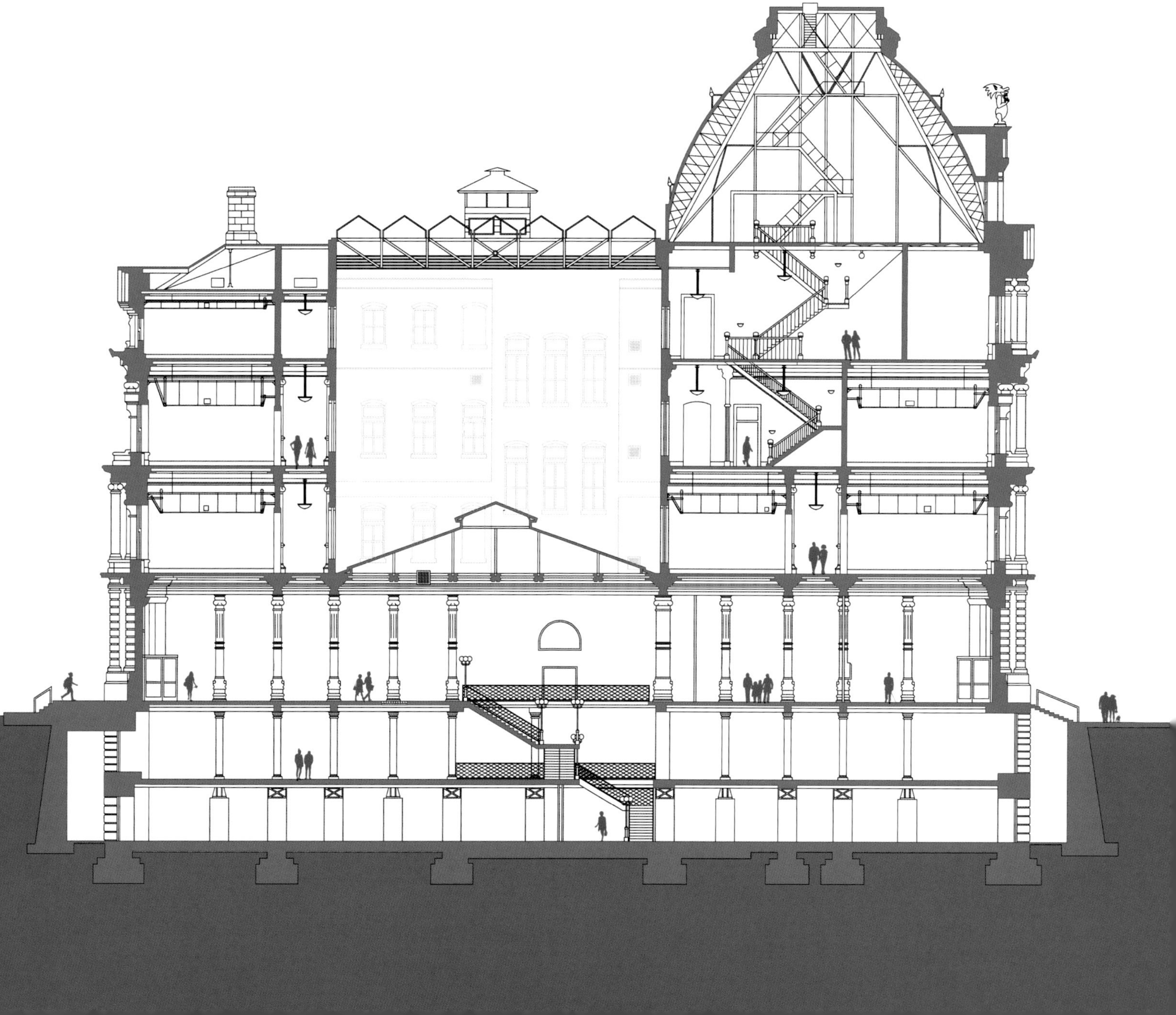

LEFT Sectional Diagram

ABOVE View of South Front and East Side of US Custom House and Old Post Office (1965)

UNITED STATES POST OFFICE AND COURT HOUS

2012 Hipolito F. Garcia Federal Building and US Courthouse

LOCATION
SAN ANTONIO, TX
DOWNTOWN

TYPE
FEDERAL

CLIENT
US GENERAL SERVICES ADMINISTRATION

Located adjacent to the historic Alamo in San Antonio, the Hipolito F. Garcia Federal Building and US Courthouse has stood as a symbol of the power and dignity of the federal government since 1937. The US General Services Administration recognized that the six-story, neoclassical, Beaux-Arts–style building, listed on the National Register of Historic Places, required renovations to improve functionality while preserving it for future generations.

GSA selected Trivers in 2004 through the Design Excellence Program as the lead architect for the restoration and renovation. The scope included site improvements, envelope restoration, accessibility and life safety compliance, tenant office renovations, and significant systems and sustainability upgrades.

A principal design goal was to seamlessly integrate historic preservation with state-of-the-art building systems and sustainability features. Throughout the design process, the team worked closely with multiple preservation organizations and advocacy groups. Restoration efforts preserved the building's extensive historic character-defining features, including lobbies, corridors, courtrooms, fixtures, ornamentation, marble wainscoting, and postal boxes. Rehabilitation of the building's exterior shell, including the historic clay tile roof, complied with the Secretary of the Interior's Standards for Rehabilitation.

Each of the building's workspaces and restrooms across 308,000 square feet was renovated, requiring the relocation of fifteen federal agency tenants.

A multiphase relocation management plan was implemented to minimize work interruption, control costs, and maintain the project schedule. Tenants moved from dark, uninspired spaces to open offices with natural light and views.

Building tenants and visitors alike appreciate the reconfigured secure entry sequence. The addition of a discreet, exterior accessible ramp and a rebuilt grand staircase featuring new flagstone paving reconnects the structure with the adjoining Alamo Plaza. Proceeding through the restored lobby, which features artist Howard Cook's sixteen-panel fresco mural depicting Texas history, visitors interact with a new stone-clad security desk and surrounding glass partitions that improve safety and circulation.

With an injection of American Recovery and Reinvestment Act funding in 2009 to help offset the economic impact of the 2008 recession, numerous sustainable features were carefully integrated into the historic structure. Highly efficient mechanical and electrical systems contributed to 50.3 percent in overall energy cost savings, while new low-flow water fixtures resulted in a 44.5 percent reduction in water use. Sixty percent of the existing interior walls, floors, and roof were reused, and half of construction waste was salvaged or recycled.

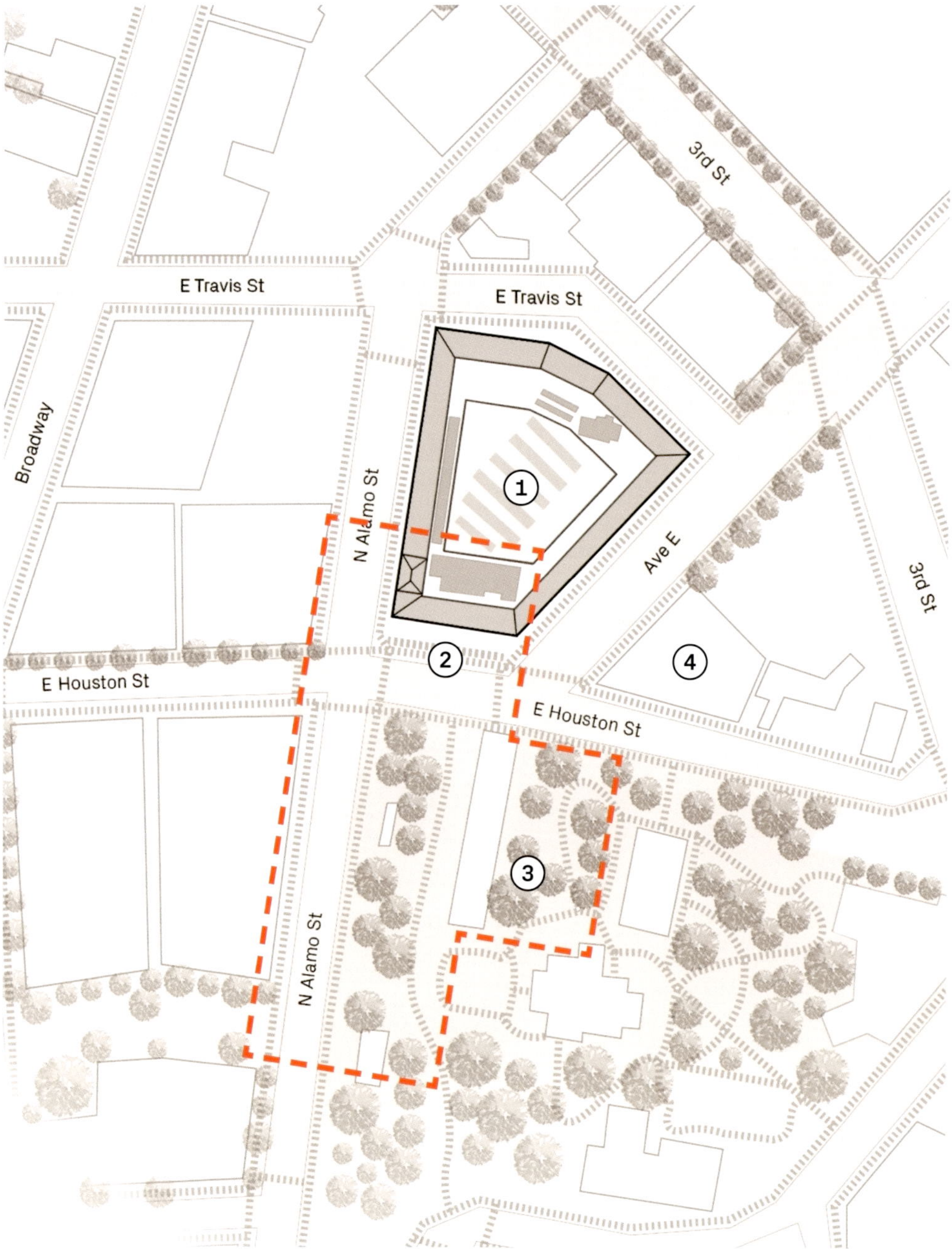

1 Hipolito F. Garcia Federal Building

2 Main Entrance

3 The Alamo

4 The Emily Morgan Hotel

- - Limits of Original Alamo Fort

The Hipolito F. Garcia building's roots are the foundation for being a leader in history, environmental stewardship and design excellence.

ENVIRONMENTAL DESIGN + CONSTRUCTION MAGAZINE

Low-emitting materials, furnishings, wood, paints, finishes, and regional and recycled materials were used throughout the tenant spaces. Outside, 95 percent of the building's shell was preserved, and a new vegetated roof was installed in the interior courtyard as an energy-conserving tenant amenity, enhancing views from the reconfigured office spaces. Upon completion in 2012, the project earned LEED Platinum certification from the US Green Building Council—a first for a GSA-owned building.

A model of collaboration between the government and private sector, the project remained under budget through cost tracking at every design phase. Not only was this a banner project for sustainability by GSA, but it also became a case study for the Texas Historical Commission, illustrating the successful integration of sustainable design within a historic structure. As one of the first federal projects to balance preservation with modern sustainability, it set a precedent for future renovations across the GSA portfolio, including later projects led by Trivers nearly two decades later.

LEFT Restored Historic Lobby

RIGHT Restored Historic Courtroom

UNITED STATES POST OFFICE AND
HOUSE

LEFT View of Hipolito F. Garcia Federal Building from Alamo Plaza

ABOVE Roof-Mounted Photovoltaic Panels

2012-2025 Gateway Arch National Park MSA

LOCATION
SAINT LOUIS, MO
DOWNTOWN

TYPE
CIVIC

CLIENT
GATEWAY ARCH
PARK FOUNDATION

Gateway Arch National Park, which includes Eero Saarinen's internationally recognized monument, its surrounding grounds, museum, and historic Old Courthouse, had long been isolated from downtown St. Louis. A depressed highway separated the Arch and park from the Old Courthouse and surrounding community. Through the largest public-private undertaking of its kind (formerly known as CityArchRiver), Gateway Arch Park Foundation and the National Park Service sought to transform the park. As winner of an international design competition, Michael Van Valkenburgh Associates developed a master plan to improve access and safety for millions of visitors. In 2012, Gateway Arch Park Foundation engaged Trivers to support several projects within the plan.

Trivers served as lead architect on twenty-four task orders under a master services agreement, focusing on the Old Courthouse, Ranger Station, and Kiener Plaza Visitor Services Center. The firm was also integral as associate architect with Cooper Robertson on the Gateway Arch Museum renovation, which included a 50,000-square-foot visitor center expansion and a new western entry to the Arch grounds. Whether designing a new building or modernizing a historic structure, Gateway Arch Park Foundation's goal of creating accessible routes, enhancing visitor experience, and improving downtown connections guided all design solutions.

The new museum and Old Courthouse create an ensemble of buildings of national significance that define a transformed public open space in downtown St. Louis. Taken together with the Arch, this will become a new destination for those interested in architecture and history, contribute to the quality of urban life for residents, and drive economic revitalization.

RETROFIT MAGAZINE, 2018

Trivers's focus on preserving the integrity of a National Historic Monument was imperative in executing these historically sensitive projects within the Dan Kiley–designed landscape. Building consensus through careful evaluation of design options ensured each project's success while supporting the master plan's broader goals. The complexity of concurrent projects required weekly design meetings with more than thirty stakeholders. Trivers also led regular reviews with the Universal Design Group, specifically evaluating accessibility improvements across all projects.

The firm's work on this collection of projects skillfully unites two centuries of historic structures with contemporary architecture, embodying in one setting the full breadth and type of expansive work created by the firm.

Visitors now easily navigate between all the park's points of interest and downtown St. Louis. The energy this connectivity has sparked continues to provide a much-needed boost to the local economy and creates an accessible, safer and more engaging experience for the millions of people who flock to Gateway Arch National Park every year as the symbol and front door to the entire St. Louis region.

KIENER PLAZA VISITOR
SERVICES CENTER
OLD COURTHOUSE
MUSEUM AT GATEWAY
ARCH NATIONAL PARK
RANGER STATION

1 Old Courthouse

2 Luther Ely Smith Square

3 Interstate

4 Gateway Arch Museum

5 Gateway Arch Rooftop Plaza

6 Railway Tunnel

7 Mississippi River

5
4
6
7

Gateway Arch National Park MSA **Ranger Station**

COMPLETION
2016

LOCATION
SAINT LOUIS, MO
DOWNTOWN

TYPE
CIVIC

CLIENT
GATEWAY ARCH
PARK FOUNDATION

For many years, the park rangers' field office was far removed from the Gateway Arch, hidden within the depths of a multi-level concrete parking deck on the park's north grounds. The Michael Van Valkenburgh Associates master plan called for reimaging the north grounds and removing this parking structure to connect the grounds to the historic Eads Bridge and Laclede's Landing. As a result, the Ranger Station required a new, more visible and accessible location.

As lead architect, Trivers worked with the National Park Service to select a new site for the station. Situated on park grounds between the existing maintenance building and commuter loop, the setting is an optimal place for law enforcement to engage in tactical operations. Now a one-and-a-half story, low-profile building set into the hillside to not obscure views of the Arch, the station is equipped with short-term detention cells, offices, a fitness center for staff, and other support spaces. The new station enhances the rangers' ability to detect and investigate violations of federal laws, apprehend and detain violators, protect life and property, and enforce all local laws and regulations with improved access and visibility.

LEFT New Entrance

ABOVE View from Pedestrian Circulator Loop

Gateway Arch National Park MSA

Gateway Arch Museum

COMPLETION
2018

LOCATION
SAINT LOUIS, MO
DOWNTOWN

TYPE
CIVIC

CLIENT
GATEWAY ARCH
PARK FOUNDATION

Trivers partnered with Cooper Robertson and James Carpenter Design Associates to expand and renovate the Museum of Westward Expansion under the Gateway Arch. Together, the designers worked to solve the constructability issues associated with creating a new subterranean structure that required high levels of security while continuing to provide public access to the National Historic Monument during construction.

The new, radiused, stainless steel and glass museum entrance mirrors the monument in its materiality and form. The new unassuming yet visible and welcoming entrance welcomes visitors to the museum through the landscape, which eventually reveals the luminous great hall and views stretching deep into the underground museum's monumentally scaled exhibits designed by London based Haley Sharpe. The existing interior was reconfigured into new galleries, public amenities, gift shop, dining, and museum staff offices. Original Saarinen designed architectural elements were preserved, and their distinctive character-defining features were highlighted with new lighting and other discrete interventions.

Saarinen's original ramps consisted of a single, uninterrupted slope leading from the base of the Arch, through the museum entrance, and into the lower level of the museum. Improvements to the ramps were designed to rest above the original ramps and provide new landings, compliant guards and handrails with detailing to protect all original historical materials. Based on Universal Design standards that exceed legal requirements, the museum is now fully accessible to people of all ages and abilities. The project has garnered more than 20 design awards and has been widely recognized in the press at local, national, and international levels.

LEFT Museum Entrance

RIGHT Museum Store and Gallery

Gateway Arch National Park MSA

Kiener Plaza Visitor Services Center

COMPLETION
2022

LOCATION
SAINT LOUIS, MO
DOWNTOWN

TYPE
CIVIC

CLIENT
GATEWAY ARCH
PARK FOUNDATION
AND
GREAT RIVERS
GREENWAY

Situated just west of the Old Courthouse grounds and outside of the National Park boundary, the city of St. Louis's Kiener Plaza was reimagined by the Michael VanValkenburg team to facilitate a more seamless connection between the Old Courthouse and downtown St. Louis, a stated goal by the Gateway Arch Park Foundation. Trivers was engaged to help select a site and design a new 600-square-foot visitor services center to accommodate the plaza's operational needs, including a permanent location for security and maintenance storage.

Working through complicated property boundaries and parcel divisions, Trivers considered sightlines, visitor circulation, and crime prevention through environmental design (CPTED) principles to select a location for the building. Purposefully playful, the center's exterior includes colorful fins that vary in orientation and change appearance as visitors move throughout the plaza. Driving more movement and activity around the building enhances safety and security for the public and park users. Integrated lighting within the fins creates a unique experience for plaza visitors at dusk and into the evening, bringing a dynamic expression to this previously darker and underutilized portion of the park. The north, west, and east concrete walls of the center provide a future canvas for murals by local artists.

The visitor services center exemplifies the thoughtful integration of design, functionality, and public engagement within an urban park setting.

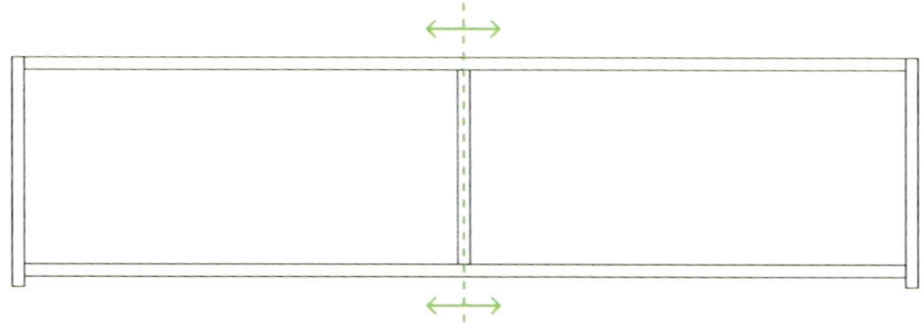

BREAK FACADE

Create better visibility for retail and security via breezeway

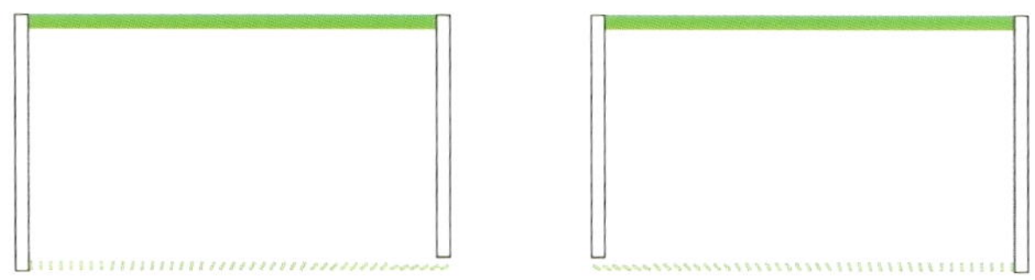

ADDRESS SITE

Street: simple / functional; Park: playful / interactive

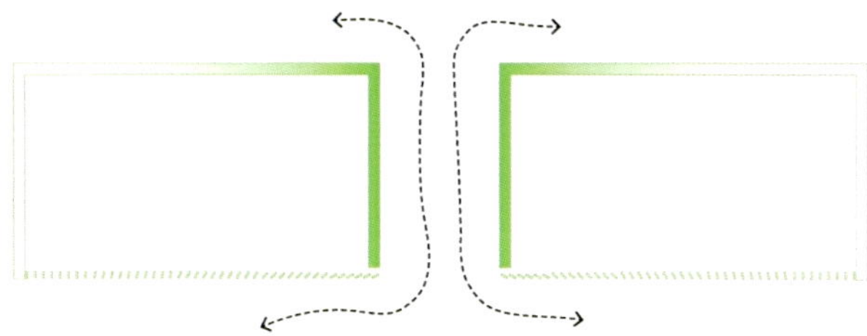

EMPHASIZE BREEZEWAY

Pull visitors through site via increasing of fins and color

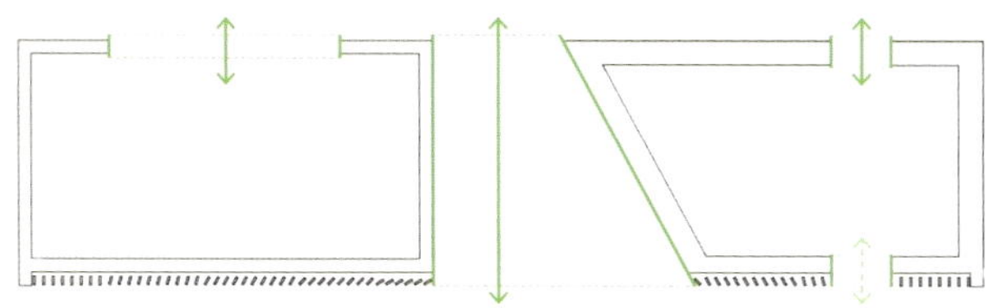

ANGLE + CONNECT

Maximize retail exposure and north-south connection

Gateway Arch National Park MSA

Old Courthouse

COMPLETION
2025

LOCATION
SAINT LOUIS, MO
DOWNTOWN

TYPE
CIVIC

CLIENT
GATEWAY ARCH
PARK FOUNDATION

One of the most consequential projects of the master plan, the Old Courthouse is historically significant for its architecture as well as events held within that shaped our nation's history. Completed before the United States Capitol in Washington, DC, the 19th-century Greek Revival structure's cast iron and copper dome was the first of its kind built in the US. Inside, the building's courtrooms are home to some of the nation's most significant court cases, including Minor v. Happersett and the 1850 Dred Scott v. Sandford case which hastened the start of The Civil War.

All design solutions required careful consideration of the potential impact on the Old Courthouse's rich historic fabric. As lead architect, Trivers conducted a full interior renovation, including museum gallery space, full mechanical system replacement, full window replacement, and installation of the building's first fire suppression system and first elevator.

Because civic buildings were intentionally elevated to increase their importance and presence, accessibility proved a challenge. Access to the building was seen as paramount to meet Universal Design standards. New exterior pedestrian ramps designed following the Secretary of the Interior's Standards for Historic Preservation allow all visitors to enter through both the east and west iconic porticos. Through careful detailing, the ramps were installed without any physical connection to the historic courthouse by utilizing a cantilevered structural design that spans the surrounding moats. For the first time in its long history, the Old Courthouse is now universally accessible to visitors of all abilities without an adverse effect to its historic fabric.

BUS
ONLY

LEFT Eastern Exterior Ramp

RIGHT Western Exterior Ramp

LEFT Rotunda Balcony

ABOVE Interior Accessibility Improvements

1908

2014 I. Jerome and Rosemary Flance Early Learning Center

LOCATION
SAINT LOUIS, MO
CARR SQUARE

TYPE
EDUCATION

CLIENT
MCCORMACK
BARON SALAZAR

For decades, the Carr Square neighborhood was the focus of comprehensive redevelopment in St. Louis. As one of Missouri's lowest-income ZIP codes, community members and neighborhood stakeholders recognized the need for a high-quality early education center that would provide life-changing opportunities for local children. In 2011, Trivers was selected as the lead architect for a pre-K educational center, and in June 2014, the I. Jerome and Rosemary Flance Early Learning Center (Flance Center) opened its doors.

Located one mile from downtown St. Louis and built on the site of one of the city's last failed International Style public housing structures, the 24,000-square-foot facility serves as both an early childhood education center and a community health care center—a unique model among childcare centers nationwide. By working extensively with residents, volunteers, and early childhood experts, Trivers created a space that addresses the needs of both children and the surrounding neighborhood.

The Flance Center carries on the legacy of Dr. I. Jerome Flance and his wife, Rosemary, who championed the principle that high-quality early childhood education and health interventions serve as the foundation for strong communities. Its operational model blends public funding sources with tuition and philanthropy, enabling an enriched experience for children from low- and moderate-income families, alongside those from families able to pay most or all tuition costs.

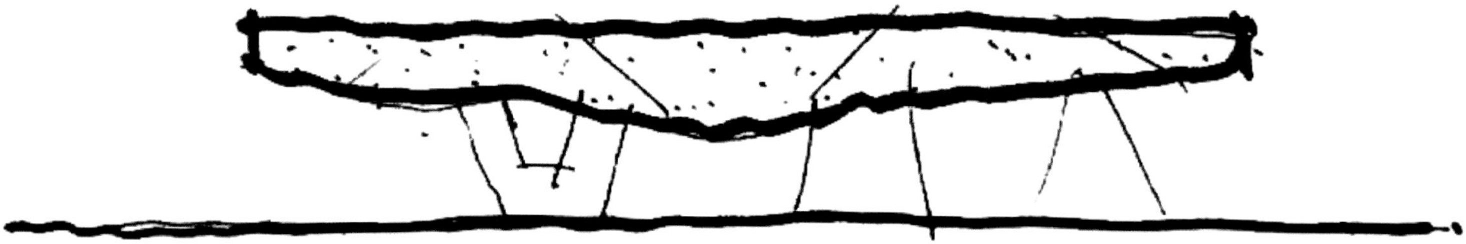

The Flance Center follows a "whole child" approach developed by leading early childhood experts at LUME Institute. This model integrates the roles of family, school, and community, providing a nurturing environment for children's emotional, social, cognitive, and physical development during their formative years, across diverse racial and socioeconomic backgrounds.

The Flance Center consists of thirteen classrooms that provide childcare and instruction to 164 children from ages six weeks to five years. Additional features include age-appropriate outdoor play spaces, community garden, dining education and full-service demonstration kitchen, classroom space for community events and faculty development, and small health care center for on-site immunizations and public health screenings.

The building's exterior serves as a protective buffer along the public street, with its massing designed to "hug" the interior-focused outdoor spaces. A perforated metal façade, inspired by a tree canopy, filters light and shades the south- and west-facing glass exposures while also providing each classroom with direct outdoor access.

Inside, a sophisticated yet playful color palette fills the space with light and energy, acting as a canvas for children to create and learn. To emphasize the importance of dietary health, the full-service and demonstration kitchen was given significant visibility within the center.

In recognition of its participatory stakeholder process and innovative design, the building received a 2017 Housing and Community Design Award from the US Department of Housing and Urban Development and the American Institute of Architects in the Community-Informed Design category. In 2021, the Flance Center was honored as a US Department of Education Green Ribbon School for its efforts to reduce environmental impact and utility costs, improve health and wellness, and ensure effective sustainability education.

The Flance Center was the capstone of reinvestment efforts that included new mixed-income housing, St. Louis Public Schools improvements, and expanded access to health care, retail, and community amenities. It has also created new employment opportunities, supporting economic development for North St. Louis residents and business owners, while also providing childcare services also used by members of Trivers's staff.

Flance was built with LEED certification in mind, and the building itself contributes to increased environmental literacy and wellness of people and the planet. It was designed to bring the outdoors in — daylighting is used in 90% of the building, every classroom has immediate access visually and physically to the outdoors.

US DEPARTMENT OF EDUCATION, GREEN RIBBON SCHOOLS

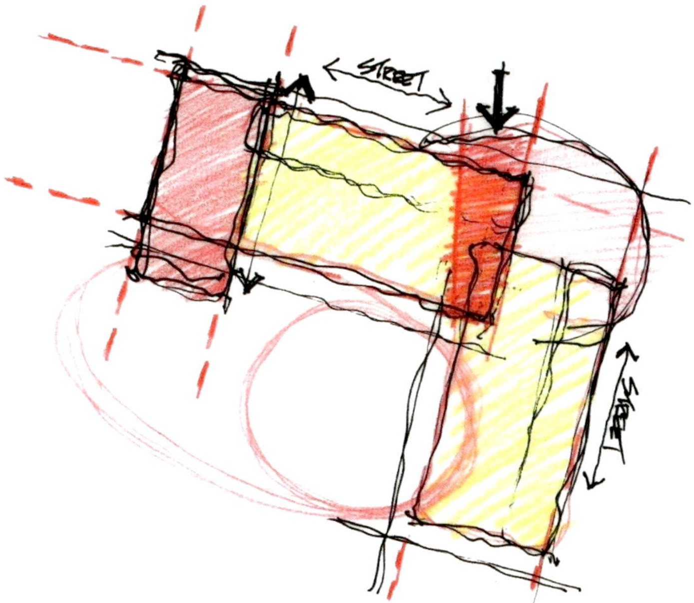

2015 Adam Aronson Fine Arts Center

LOCATION
SAINT LOUIS COUNTY, MO
SUNSET HILLS

TYPE
CIVIC

CLIENT
LAUMEIER
SCULPTURE PARK

Located on the edge of suburban St. Louis and rural Missouri, Laumeier Sculpture Park is an icon of the arts in the St. Louis region. Renowned as one of the oldest, largest, and most prestigious open-air museums, Laumeier attracts more than 350,000 visitors annually, who come from around the world to marvel at 70 large-scale outdoor sculptures across its 105-acre grounds.

To display artwork year-round in a controlled environment and enhance its ability to provide high-quality learning experiences, Laumeier selected Trivers to design the new Adam Aronson Fine Arts Center (AAFAC) and park entry plaza. The firm was also commissioned to renovate the original Estate House-the only indoor public structure on the park's property—into the Kranzberg Education Lab. Constructed in 1917, the Estate House had played a role in essential park functions such as art storage and served as the welcome center, museum shop, and staff offices. However, the scale, proportions, and physical limitations of the original construction offered little to no space for new programming and events, and the unpredictability of the outdoors made exhibiting climate-sensitive art a challenge.

Drawing inspiration from the area's farming history and artistic identity, Trivers created the AAFAC, a 7,500-square-foot building with striking features reminiscent of the iconic art dispersed around Laumeier. Named in honor of the park's co-founder, the building is perched on a plinth adjacent to the Estate

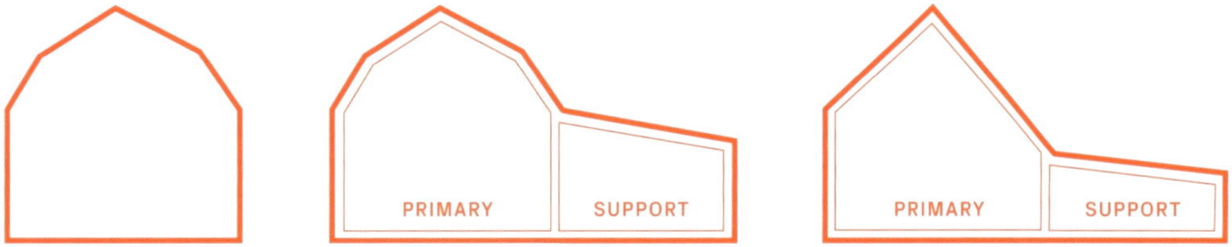

Gambrel Barn | Gambrel Barn with Lean-To Shed | Modified Gambrel

House, demonstrating its significance while also deferring to the historic structure.

The AAFAC's exterior features western red cedar siding and a metal roof, evoking the contrast between the park's steel sculptures and their natural backdrops. Large windows line the front of the building, while strategically placed wooden slats prevent sunlight from striking the gallery walls and damaging the artwork.

Although the building's barnlike form evokes the site's agrarian past, its design is also practical. The open, expansive volume of the interior allows for flexibility, creating new opportunities for art exhibits, special events, and revenue-generating functions. The AAFAC also includes park visitor restrooms, a gift shop, and other support spaces such as art collection storage, a space for art conservation, event facilities, and a catering kitchen.

Moving gallery functions to the AAFAC enabled the transformation of the Estate House into the Kranzberg Education Lab. The first floor features spacious areas for educational classes, lectures, and workshops, permitting year-round programming for visitors of all ages, regardless of the weather. The building provides rental spaces for meetings and events while housing the park offices on the second floor.

The construction of the AAFAC, alongside the reimagined Kranzberg Education Lab, has transformed the site into a dynamic, multiuse public space that fosters human connection in an increasingly fragmented world. While the Estate House once served as a retreat from the bustling city, the AAFAC is designed to bring people together, using art as a catalyst for shared experiences. The project was recognized with multiple honors, including an award from AIA Central States and two from AIA St. Louis. These shared spaces stand as a testament to the enduring relationship between art, nature, and human connection.

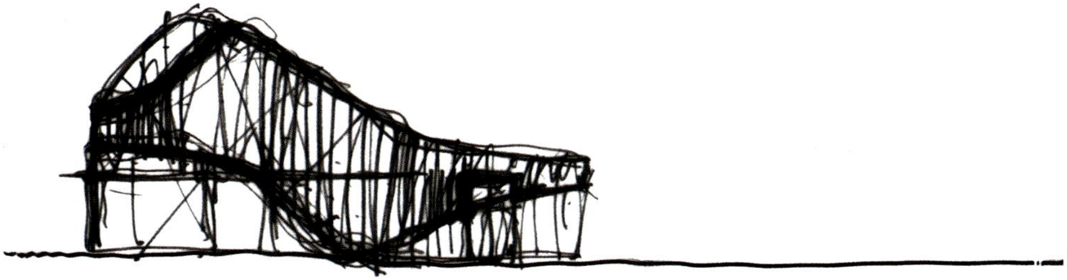

We really take a lot of pride in how it refers to place. For years to come the center will contribute to the park's mission, allowing artists to show off different methods for creating work and using the space in a dramatic way. I think people just can't believe how beautiful this little piece of architecture is.

MARILU KNODE, EXECUTIVE DIRECTOR, LAUMEIER SCULPTURE PARK
***ST. LOUIS MAGAZINE,* 2015**

ABOVE Lobby Reception

RIGHT Whitaker Foundation Gallery

2017 UPIKE Health Professions Education Building

LOCATION
PIKEVILLE, KY
DOWNTOWN

TYPE
HIGHER EDUCATION

CLIENT
UNIVERSITY
OF PIKEVILLE

The University of Pikeville (UPIKE) has been in the heart of Kentucky coal country since 1889. Pikeville, population 7,500, is situated in a narrow river valley in mountainous Pike County, near the West Virginia border. Its remote location, rugged terrain, and lack of connection to the interstate make much of the area and UPIKE's campus difficult to access. The renowned Hatfield and McCoy feud was the town's claim to fame until 1987, when the Pikeville Cut-Through rerouted the Levisa Fork of the Big Sandy River and the adjoining railroad to mitigate annual flooding and persistent coal dust downtown. Moving 18 million cubic yards of sediment—second only to the Panama Canal in excavation projects-instilled a belief that anything can be built anywhere.

As the world shifts away from fossil fuels to cleaner energy, UPIKE's leadership recognized the need for central Appalachian youth to receive a high-quality education to thrive in the health and technology sectors of a 21st-century economy. Along with a desire for economic mobility, UPIKE's leadership envisioned the Health Professions Education Building as a resource for both the university and the greater Appalachian community. The Pikeville region is among the most underserved in vision care, with the population decimated by sight loss linked to malnutrition associated with type 2 diabetes.

Designed by Trivers in partnership with Associate Architect Ayers Saint Gross, the building was sited on one of the last open parcels of land on campus—a 45 degree slope with an

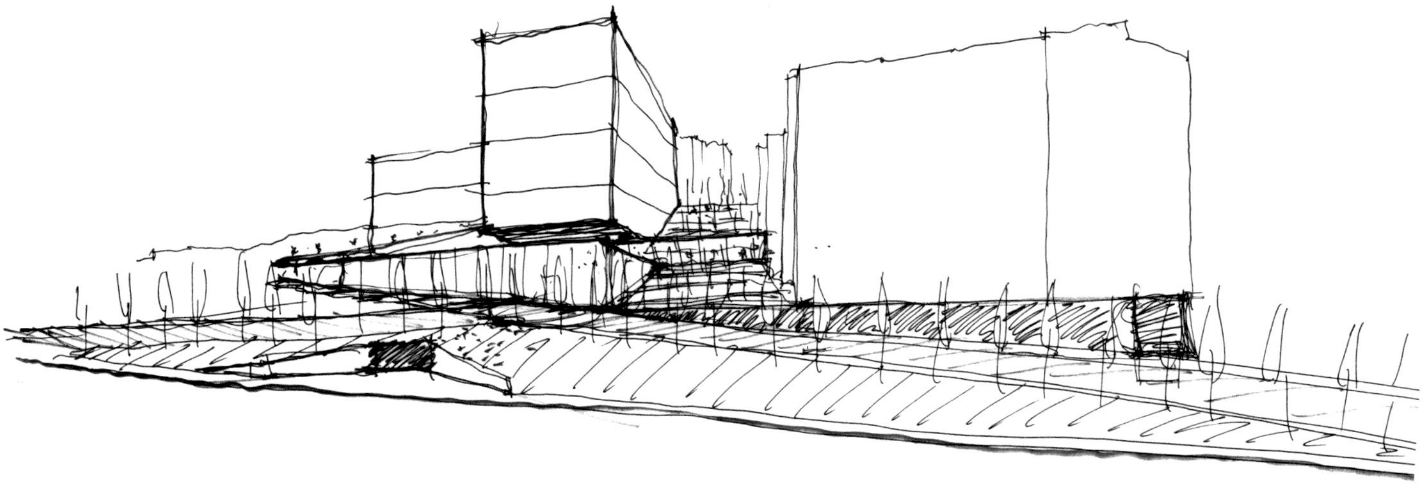

80-foot vertical change—a surmountable challenge for a population that once rerouted a river. With the campus above and town below, the site also allowed the new Health Professions facility to connect to the School of Nursing. Enhancing the pedestrian street along the building's north elevation creates a new sense of place, promoting student interaction and leading to the campus center—connected to the "99" steps ascending from town to campus.

Programmatically, the building houses active learning classrooms and optometry labs aligned with the nation's top programs. It features collaborative and study areas, faculty offices, an assembly space for both university and community, student dining open to the public, and a multiuse, clear-span pavilion with commanding views of the Appalachian Mountains, all unified by a vertical core that physically and symbolically connects campus to town.

The structure both respects and defies the slope—a testament to Pikeville's ability to conquer difficult terrain through innovation, creativity, and technical excellence. The building envelope melds dark grays and blacks of Appalachian vernacular with etched glazing that evokes striations of excavated bedrock. A primary façade feature, these glass "layers of clarity" serve as an emblematic design statement for the Kentucky College of Optometry. The project has been recognized with multiple honors, including Merit Awards from both AIA Kentucky and AIA St. Louis, and was named Optometry School of the Year by the National Optometric Association.

Former UPIKE president and governor of Kentucky Paul Patton stated in 2012, "If you teach them in the mountains, they will stay in the mountains." An educated workforce has been emerging through the Health Professions Education Building for nearly a decade, equipping students with skills to drive economic growth and create jobs in this isolated region. Since its first class completed the program in 2020, 280 students have graduated.

In addition to advancing UPIKE's mission of expanding academic opportunities, the Health Professions Education Building provides much-needed medical services. To help alleviate vision impairment, an optometry clinic operated by students is open to the public, further activating the building with students and patients alike.

Since 2016, UPIKE has added a College of Nursing and Human Services and a College of Dental Medicine. The Health Professions Education Building symbolizes the mobility quality education provides and stands as a beacon of UPIKE's prominence in central Appalachia and beyond.

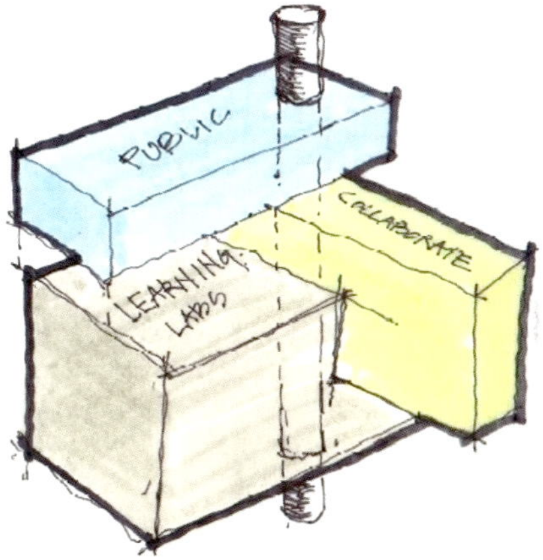

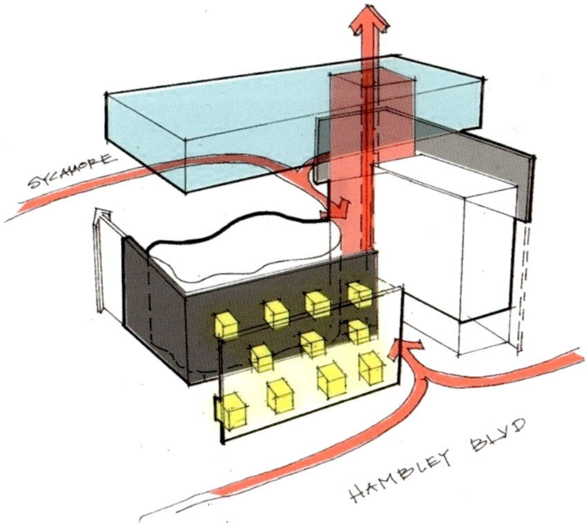

TOP RIGHT Conceptual Programmatic Diagram

BOTTOM RIGHT Conceptual Circulation and Programmatic Diagram

LEFT Sectional Diagram

ABOVE References to Historic Landscapes that Influenced the Design

Estimate the Angle

It is one thing to have exceptional architectural design which supports the intent of the users of a building. [Trivers'] work on the Kentucky College of Optometry has done nothing short of having a profound effect on the entire program.

DR. ANDREW BUZZELLI, OD, MS,
FOUNDING DEAN, KENTUCKY COLLEGE OF OPTOMETRY

2019 **Woodward Lofts**

LOCATION
SAINT LOUIS, MO
THE GROVE

TYPE
MULTI-FAMILY

CLIENT
PIER PROPERTY GROUP

Originally constructed in the 1920s as a commercial printing facility for Woodward & Tiernan Printing Company, Woodward Lofts, located in St. Louis's Grove neighborhood, stands as a monument to the prominence of the commercial printing industry in St. Louis and the evolution of industrial factory design in the early 20th century. Its features, including five clerestory monitors for innovative daylighting, helped the structure earn a spot on the National Register of Historic Places in 2014.

The building's developer partnered with Trivers in 2016 to adapt the 235,000-square-foot structure, which at the time was only sparingly used as a warehouse and distribution center for packaging materials. The goal was to honor the original beauty and character of the building while also creating a livable community for future residents on the edge of a burgeoning neighborhood.

Leveraging its largest defining features—the five clerestory monitors and robust floors—the renovation was designed to be addition by subtraction, removing roofs and floor slabs to create daylit courtyards with loft-style living. Ultimately, 164 loft-style apartments were created, utilizing an open floor plan, soaring clerestory monitors, and dramatic steel-sash window openings. High-performance glazing was used in the aluminum replica windows to reduce heat gain and glare while still complying with the Secretary of the Interior's Standards for Rehabilitation. The building's original entrance and east end were made accessible once again and now host street frontage retail and tenant amenities that feature original oak and leaded-glass office partitions.

Vestiges of the printing factory are incorporated throughout Woodward Lofts, including remnants of a rail spur that allowed boxcars to be loaded directly from the factory floor. A portion of the building's sprinkler tank room was adapted into a rooftop lounge that opens to a rooftop deck and pool with views of St. Louis's skyline beyond. The interior design includes a dark, inky color palette, mid twentieth-century furniture pieces, and artwork inspired by original typesetting procedures, a homage to the building's origin. The concrete and steel structure contained nearly 11,000-metric-tons of embodied carbon. With sustainability in mind, the design team retained as much of the original building as possible but also strategically removed portions to increase its usability. Former loading docks on the north and west façades were replaced with landscaped entries to create a welcoming arrival sequence, and courtyards shared by up to ten units each were carved between the original monitors.

Additionally, utilizing cross-laminated timber (CLT) floors for lofts within units created a total carbon benefit of 376-metric-tons over traditional floor assembly. CLT also reduced the floor thickness by nearly twelve inches over

BEFORE + AFTER
Restored Grand Stair

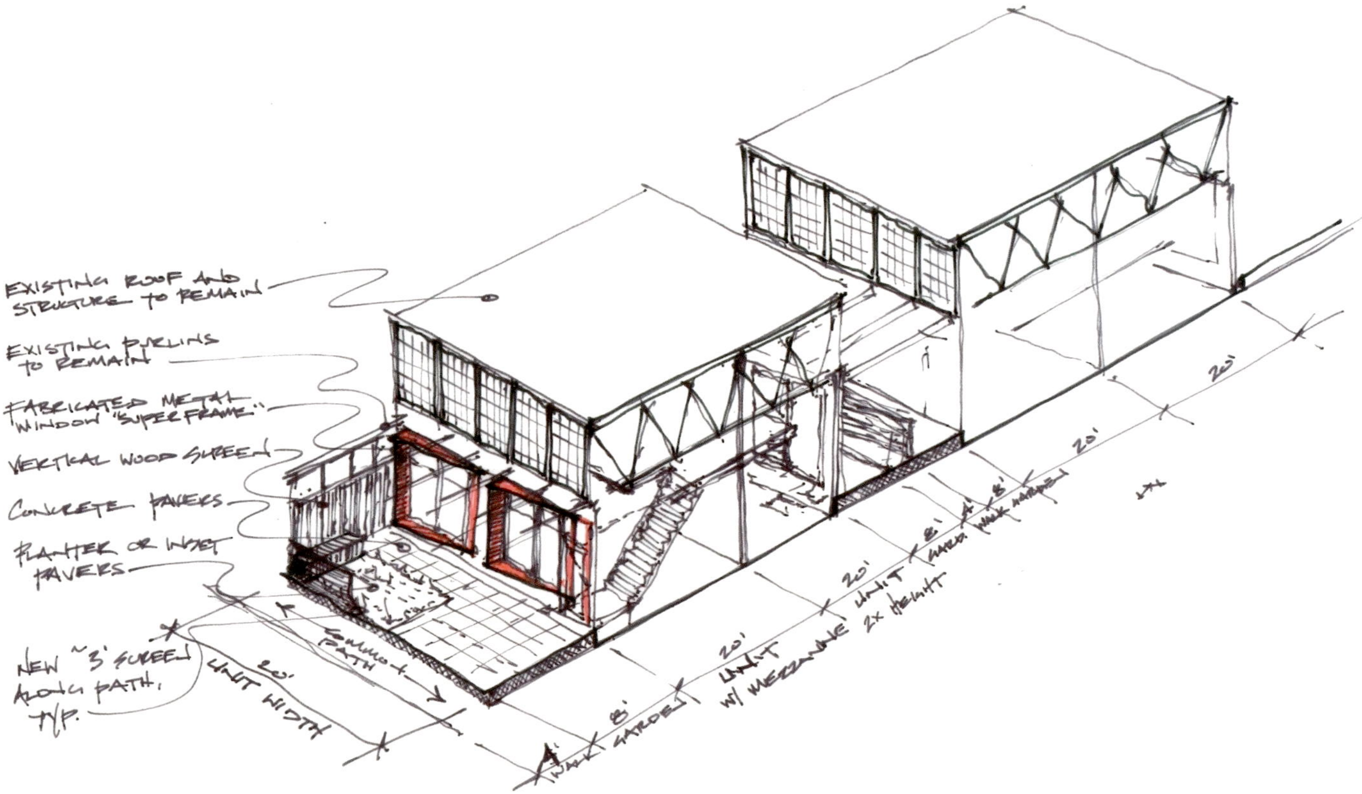

conventional framing, which maintained a viable head height in the newly created lofted bedrooms while mitigating the length of stair runs to save valuable floor space below. A surprising discovery revealed that the original factory floors were a dark, monolithic terrazzo obscured by years of dirt. Cleaning, patching, and polishing the original floors further minimized the use of new construction materials across nearly 200,000 square feet.

Woodward Lofts was named a winner of the 2023 American Institute of Architects Housing Awards, which annually recognizes ten exceptional residential designs throughout the United States. It also received a Metamorphosis Award in the multifamily category from *Retrofit Magazine*, a Palladio Award in the residential category from *Traditional Building Magazine*, and an Honor Award from the St. Louis AIA Chapter, and a Preserve Missouri Award from *Missouri Preservation*.

The building's redevelopment has catalyzed the construction of new affordable and market-rate infill housing in the surrounding blocks. Serving as a significant bookend to the Grove neighborhood, the project reactivates a long-underutilized asset at one of the city's fastest-growing intersections. Rooted in historic industrial architecture, it is a home unique to its place, bridging past and present.

The architect's use of section and exterior voids creates distinctive social spaces and intriguing relationships between neighbors. In addition, the existing building's form, materials and details were reused extremely well, producing a unique building that evokes yet transcends its past. The use of cross-laminated timber (CLT) in the interior is a key component that elevates the environmental quality of this adaptive reuse.

AIA ST. LOUIS JURY COMMENT

LEFT Concept Sketch

RIGHT Typical Residential Corridor

ABOVE Cross-laminated Timber (CLT)
Installation at Residential Unit Interior

Vandeventer
SHOWCASE STL

TOP Finishing Department + Print Factory Inspiration

BOTTOM Longitudinal Building Section

BEFORE + AFTER Main Entrance

BEFORE + AFTER West Approach

2

ABOVE Rooftop Sky Lounge and Typical Unit

2021 Tower Grove Park Pavilions

LOCATION
SAINT LOUIS, MO
TOWER GROVE

TYPE
CIVIC

CLIENT
TOWER GROVE PARK

Widely regarded as the best and most complete example of 19th-century urban park design remaining in the United States, Tower Grove Park in St. Louis is one of only seven parks designated as a National Historic Landmark. By providing recreational, educational, and cultural opportunities, the park serves as an anchor and economic stabilizer for several surrounding historic neighborhoods and business districts.

The park boasts the largest collection of Victorian pavilions in the world, which helped it earn a spot on the National Register of Historic Places. Each pavilion, designed and constructed between 1870 and 1873, features a unique, ornamental design with intricate detailing and vibrant paint colors. Well-loved and in constant use, these one-of-a-kind pavilions had begun to show extensive structural and cosmetic deterioration as they approached their 150th year.

Tower Grove Park selected Trivers to renovate and restore the iconic Turkish Pavilion and Old Playground Pavilion. After the design team's initial assessment, observations revealed several challenges, including accessibility issues, water infiltration, and material decay. Structural concerns were also apparent, such as stress fractures in the wrought-iron columns at the Turkish Pavilion and both isolated and extensive wood column deterioration at the Old Playground Pavilion, along with inadequate and failing footings at both sites.

BELOW Historic Photo of the Turkish Pavilion Completed in 1872

Restoration for each pavilion required meticulous interventions. The design team outlined the scope of work and relied heavily on skilled carpenters to recreate the pavilions' original details based on adjacent historic materials.

Both pavilions received structural improvements to their wood columns, including custom shoring to accommodate the delicate roof structural systems and new concrete footings poured beneath them. The design team added exposed concrete slabs beyond the roof edge, improving accessibility and easing maintenance for the surrounding lawns by enhancing directional drainage.

Another unique repair included nickel-based peened welding at the cast-iron columns of the Turkish Pavilion. The air-hammer peening process involved striking and spreading nickel-based weld beads while slowing the cooling rate with insulating blankets. This process minimized stress on the cast iron as it cooled—an uncommon and intricate construction practice in the modern era.

Deteriorating terneplate areas were patched using compatible metal and historically appropriate techniques, ensuring the long-term preservation of the original terne-metal roof material. The roof was covered with a polyurethane-modified methyl methacrylate coating, and custom colors were specified to match the original pavilion paint. Strategically placed lighting now allows the pavilions to be viewed after dusk, resulting in a museum-like display. In the darkness, allowing these jewels to now shine.

Restored to their original Victorian beauty in 2021, the Turkish Pavilion and Old Playground Pavilion represent the park's initial investment in preserving its collection of treasures. Trivers continues to work with the park to restore the remaining pavilions, ensuring they each remain safe, accessible, and well-equipped to inspire and host visitors for generations to come.

TURKISH PAVILION
1872
RESERVED TODAY
Coming soon

St. Louis's Tower Grove Park, one of only seven parks designated as a National Historic Landmark, has the greatest collection of Victorian pavilions in the world.

BEFORE + AFTER
Old Playground Pavilion

LEFT + RIGHT
Restored Old Playground Pavilion

S
E
W
N

2023 DOORWAYS

LOCATION
SAINT LOUIS, MO
JEFF-VANDER-LOU

TYPE
MULTI-FAMILY
NON-PROFIT

CLIENT
DOORWAYS

"Out of the Darkness and Into the Light" was the guiding vision in planning and designing DOORWAYS' transformative new campus. An interfaith nonprofit organization, DOORWAYS is a national model providing housing and supportive services for those battling homelessness or unstable housing, poverty, and poor health because of HIV.

Due to the stigma long associated with HIV, DOORWAYS was originally based in an inconspicuous structure, hidden within St. Louis's Central West End neighborhood. To help eliminate bias surrounding HIV, remove access barriers, and create a network of support for clients, DOORWAYS decided on a new, centralized, highly visible campus along North Jefferson Avenue—one of the most traveled north-south corridors in St. Louis.

Critical to the project's success and DOORWAYS' internal streamlining, multiple charrettes attended by current and past DOORWAYS clients, employees, board members, community participants, and the design team yielded the vision for a modern, cutting-edge campus that is also warm and welcoming for all.

The project was conceptualized in two phases, allowing funding to align with availability. Phase One implemented a 16,000-square-foot building offering client services and programming facilities alongside administrative offices and support. Allen House, an adjoining 45,000-square-foot, multi-story wing with fifty residential units housing up to 112 people per night, was designed as emergency housing for unhoused individuals affected by HIV.

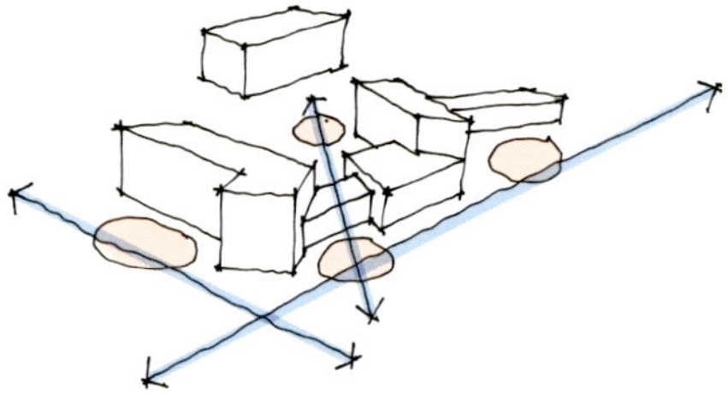

Elliott Place, a thirty-nine-unit, 31,000-square-foot permanent housing building, was constructed shortly thereafter in Phase Two to complement Allen House. Elliott Place empowers clients to move on to a more stable, independent living situation while continuing to receive vital support from DOORWAYS and its community partners, including behavioral health counseling, a provisions pantry, employment assistance, medical case management, and self-development classes.

A dedicated pharmacy, constructed in Phase Two serves both the DOORWAYS campus and the greater community as a retail pharmacy. Strategically positioned in a pharmacy desert, it fills a significant void in pharmaceutical services for the neighborhood. A future phase will add a drop-in clinic, further enhancing the campus's role as a health hub where DOORWAYS clients and community members can receive medication management guidance and other essential health services.

With the design and construction of each piece of the new campus, sustainability remained a focus. Advanced wood framing techniques, known as optimum-value engineering (OVE), increased energy efficiency while reducing lumber consumption and construction waste. Landscaped stormwater bioretention zones filter and absorb runoff in a city with antiquated infrastructure prone to flooding. Carefully considered tree groves provide shading, reducing solar intensity on the building and, in turn, cooling loads and energy use while enhancing views for residents. The project's 18-percent reduction in energy use intensity (EUI) enabled it to achieve Enterprise Green Communities certification.

Fostering a social atmosphere and encouraging community interaction, the campus includes a mix of private and public outdoor spaces. New infrastructure improves access to the adjacent neighborhood and nearby schools, all oriented around the campus's outward-facing public plaza and integrated transit stop. Designed in partnership with St. Louis's Gateway Foundation as a landmark for public art and social consciousness, the plaza features *Rumors of War*, a sculpture by renowned artist Kehinde Wiley that reimagines Confederate equestrian statues—portraying African Americans with empowerment rather than victimization. Selected to reflect both the organization's mission to provide housing and support for those in need and St. Louis's ongoing struggle with racism, the artwork anchors the primary residential entrance with a powerful visual statement.

DOORWAYS' campus represents one of the largest investments in North St. Louis in decades. As an organization that has long supported disinvested communities, DOORWAYS' new campus serves as a central node for the region, inspiring people affected by HIV to come out of the shadows and serving as a resource that helps them not only survive but succeed and pursue their dreams.

DOORWAYS
RESTROOMS

DOORWAYS
35 YEARS
DOORWAYS
HOPE LIVES HERE
35 YEARS
DOORWAYS
HOPE LIVES HERE

Trivers took the time to get to know not only our agency and mission but the people behind it all, from the board to staff and clients. The team learned our DNA and that is how they designed a building that not only meets our needs but anticipated how we might grow in the future.

TODD GARTEN
VICE PRESIDENT OF OPERATIONS, DOORWAYS

LEFT Planting Areas Outside Public Facing Residential Units

TOP RIGHT Aerial View of Gathering Area

BOTTOM RIGHT Gathering Space Outside Private Residences

THE VICTOR
Opening Summer 2023
Pre-Leasing
victorstl.com
BREAKFAST
CHILI
BURGERS
COFFEE
ONE TASTE AND YOU'RE HOOKED

2023 The Victor

LOCATION
SAINT LOUIS, MO
DOWNTOWN WEST

TYPE
MULTI-FAMILY

CLIENT
DEVELOPMENT
SERVICES GROUP

Before Costco and Amazon, the Butler Brothers warehouse-distribution building, constructed in 1906, stood as the modern wholesaler of its day. The 735,000-square-foot structure sat vacant for nearly three decades before Trivers was commissioned by DSG to revitalize this sleeping giant. Located in St. Louis's Downtown West neighborhood, adjacent to the newly built St. Louis CITY SC soccer stadium, the building's sheer scale, long dormancy, and potential to catalyze surrounding development made it an ideal candidate for transformation.

The building's size was both an asset and a challenge to its redevelopment. The largest monolithic reinforced concrete structure west of the Mississippi River at the time of its construction, its load-bearing brick masonry perimeter walls and early fire protection system enabled it to endure for more than a century. Yet, this same robustness left much of the interior unchanged, even as the building sat largely vacant for decades.

At its core, this project embodies the interplay between old and new, past and future. Preserving as much of the original structure as possible maintained its legacy while breathing new life into it. Decades of coal soot were removed, revealing the exterior brick and Missouri pink granite in their original splendor. The building's remaining terra cotta cornice was carefully restored, while the original clamshell-style garage doors—once used for horse-drawn wagons—were preserved and permanently fixed in place. Elements of the building's rich history were also incorporated throughout the interior, including patterns and color palettes inspired by early 20th-century fashion trends. Chess motifs reference the site's inclusion in the Washington Avenue Historic District and its ties to Harmonie Hall, which hosted the first-ever World Chess Championship in 1886.

Because of the project's eligibility for state and federal historic tax credits, it was designed in accordance with the National Park Service guidelines for historic structures. Spatially, the building was reorganized along a dominant east-west axis, with 17th Street leading to a new resident lobby, an open courtyard, and the original 18th Street entry, now accessed via a newly designed monumental stair and enclosure. One of the most substantial architectural moves was the removal of the eastern courtyard wall to increase daylight penetration and create twenty-four additional viable units, all while maintaining a seamless material relationship with the historic exterior. Apartment units and tenant amenities were strategically arranged along this new axis, reactivating the building from within.

The Victor now features 384 apartments along with high-end amenities, including an expansive rooftop terrace with a pool, pickleball court, sundeck, and dog park.

BEFORE + AFTER
Stair Enclosure and Passive Courtyard

EXIT
EXIT

Encircling the newly expanded light court, a fitness center with dedicated yoga and pilates studios, a golf simulator, lounges, work-from-home offices, and an internal parking garage provide modern conveniences tailored to contemporary urban living. Each space reflects a layered transformation, telling the story of the building's evolving purpose and the people who have inhabited it.

In a time when quality attainable housing is increasingly out of reach, intentional unit variation ensures a range of price points, making rental rates more accessible. The building's scale allowed for a variety of unit layouts, responding to different elevations and exposures. With an average apartment size of 943-square-feet (88-square-meters), The Victor offers larger living spaces than the national average, enhancing residents' quality of life and countering the trend toward smaller units.

The project demonstrates how leveraging a community's existing built environment can provide much-needed quality housing. It exemplifies how adaptive reuse preserves architectural heritage while also supporting environmental sustainability. Repurposing the building's concrete and masonry significantly reduced environmental impact, eliminating

BEFORE + AFTER
Restored Historic 18th Street Lobby

the need for carbon-intensive material extraction and production. The 23,988 short tons (21,760 metric tonnes) of embodied carbon within the Victor represent a footprint that, if replicated today, would take St. Louis's Forest Park another 100 years to offset.

The Victor has been recognized with multiple honors, including a 2025 American Institute of Architects Housing Award, as well as a Distinguished Award in Preservation and Adaptive Reuse from AIA St. Louis, a Citation Award in Architecture from AIA Central States, and a Preserve Missouri Award from *Missouri Preservation*.

In May 2024, Trivers became a proud resident of the Victor, relocating from its home of nearly thirty years to a new 8,000-square-foot office on the building's ground floor. This move not only provided the opportunity to work in an open, flexible environment designed specifically for the firm's needs but also served as a direct commitment to revitalizing downtown St. Louis. By occupying and activating the street level, Trivers contributes to the energy and vibrancy essential to a thriving urban core.

It is rare for a single project to transform an entire city block. Where a dark, vacant structure once loomed over the surrounding streets, there is now light, life, and renewed purpose.

> Adaptive reuse poses a series of puzzles in typological thinking, and Trivers has played the game at an advanced level.
>
> ***ARCHITECTURAL RECORD*, 2024**

LEFT Original Materials and Details that Influenced the Building's Renewed Design

RIGHT Restored Exterior Facade

ABOVE Historic Artwork and Photos that Influenced Design

LEFT Elevator Lobby and Mailroom

BEFORE + AFTER
Monumental Stair

BEFORE + AFTER
Lounge & Game Room

bank
SAINT LOUIS UNIVERSITY

Timeline

1975 – Founded as SRT Architects and Planners

1976 – Completes first project: Washington Apartments with McCormack Baron

1980 – Wins first design award for Bridgeton Community Center

1982 – Begins work on first Washington University project

19
92
–
Grand Center Master Plan receives Progressive Architecture Award

19
95
–
Moves to 100 North Broadway in downtown St. Louis

–
Completes first American Cancer Society project

20
03
–
Wins first local AIA award for Sisters of St. Joseph of Carondelet Holy Family Chapel

19
83
–
Renamed Trivers Associates, Inc.

19
94
–
Secures first United States General Services Administration (GSA) project (IDIQ 1994-1999)

20
05
–
Opens Illinois office

2007

6 North Apartments receives John M. Clancy Award for Socially Responsible Housing, is featured in The New York Times, and becomes the first large-scale multifamily project incorporating Universal Design

2010

Woolworth Building awarded Contract Magazine's Inspiration Award

Grice-Trivers Joint Venture formed

2008

Recognized as one of the Top 100 Fastest-Growing Inner-City Companies by Inc. Magazine

The Old Post Office selected for AIA Justice Facilities Review

The City Hall of University City becomes Missouri's first LEED-certified municipal building

2011

Andy Trivers elevated to AIA College of Fellows

2012

Joe Brinkmann named president

Hipolito F. Garcia Federal Building becomes GSA's first LEED Platinum project

2014

Completes first One Plus pro bono project: St. Louis ArtWorks

2017

Flance Early Learning Center wins AIA/HUD Secretary's Award for Community-Informed Design

Firm signs AIA 2030 Commitment

2013

Southern Illinois University Edwardsville (SIUE) Art & Design Building becomes campus' first LEED Gold project

Trivers acquires Tec Plus

2015

Ownership transitions from founder Andy Trivers to Joe Brinkmann, Joel Fuoss, and Amy Gilbertson

3010 Apartments receives National Trust/HUD Secretary's Award for Excellence in Historic Preservation

2018

Trivers's team member presents at the AIA Conference on Architecture for the first time, followed by six additional speakers to date

Gateway Arch Museum completed, wins 20+ design awards, and is featured on the cover of Architectural Record

2019

- Establishes Interior Design department
- Amy Gilbertson becomes one of the first Fitwel Ambassadors in the U.S.
- Firm requires all design staff to obtain LEED credentials
- Recognized as an Emerging Professional Friendly Firm (EPFF) by AIA Central States, with Outstanding EPFF distinction in 2022

2022

- Amy Gilbertson elevated to AIA College of Fellows
- Completes smallest project to date—Kiener Plaza Visitor Services Center (600 SF), recognized with an AIA St. Louis Distinguished Award for Small Project

2024

- Names two Associate Principals: Neil Chace and Martin Padilla
- Headquarters moved to the Victor in downtown St. Louis

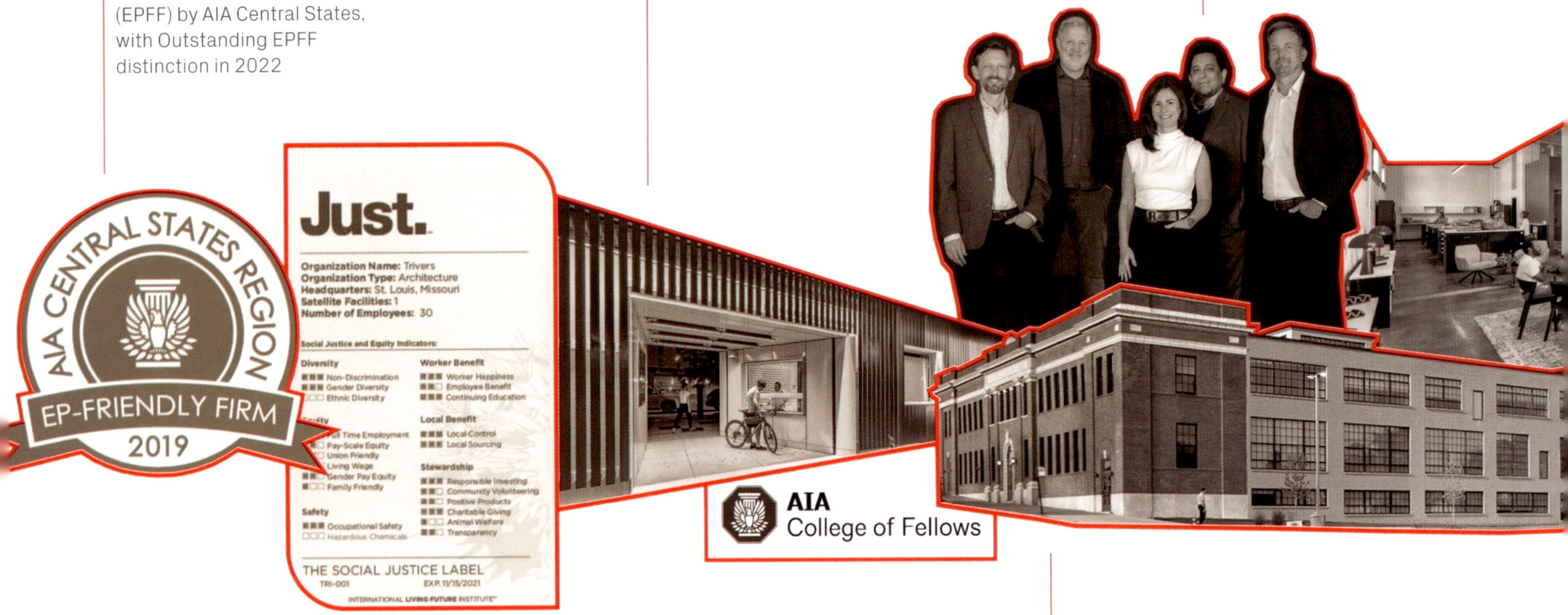

2020

- Earns first JUST label

2023

- Wins national AIA Housing Award for Woodward Lofts

As we mark fifty years of creativity, dedication, and design excellence, we honor the legacy we've built — and embrace the challenges and opportunities ahead. Our commitment to solving complex problems, advancing sustainable solutions, and driving meaningful change remains unwavering. The next chapter of our story will be shaped by our passion for creating spaces that inspire, connect, and transform communities.

2025

– Wins national AIA Housing Award for The Victor

– Celebrates 50th anniversary

– Publishes *A Legacy of Positive Consequence*

Credits

McCormack Baron Salazar Partnership
Photo Credits: Sam Fentress, *pages 19-21* | Photo courtesy of McCormack Baron Salazar, *page 22*

Washington University Partnership
Photo Credits: Sam Fentress, *pages 25, 27* | ©Brad Feinkopf, *page 26* | Alise O'Brien, *pages 27-29*

American Cancer Society Partnership
Photo Credits: Sam Fentress

US General Services Administration Partnership
Photo Credits: Courtesy of the US General Services Administration, *page 37* | Library of Congress, Prints & Photographs Division, photograph by Carol M. Highsmith, *page 38* |
Mark Menjivar, *page 39* | Sam Fentress, *page 40*

Grice Group Architects Partnership
Photo Credits: Sam Fentress, *pages 43-44, 46* | Allen Ahner *page 45* | Photos courtesy of McCormack Baron Salazar, *page 45*

The Westin
Collaborators: Trivers, *architect* | Thomas Gilbertson & Associates, Inc., *MEP/T engineer* | ABS Consulting, *structural engineer* | EDM, Inc., *civil engineer* | Anderson/Miller, Ltd., *interior design* | Austin Tao & Associates, Inc., *landscape architecture* | Randy Burkett Lighting Design, *lighting design* | John J. Urbikas & Associates, *vertical transportation* | Brinkmann Construction, *General Contractor*
Project Awards & Recognition: Excellence in Masonry, Rehab/Restoration/Addition Award, Distinction in Craftsmanship, *Masonry Institute of St. Louis* | Honor Award, Preservation Week, *Landmarks Association of St. Louis* | Missouri Historic Preservation Tax Credit Project Award, *Missouri Downtown Association*
Photo Credits: Robert Pettus, *page 50* | Sam Fentress, *pages 53, 55* | Alise O'Brien, *page 54*

6 North Apartments
Collaborators: Trivers, *architect, interior design* | Case Engineering (Ædifica) *MEP/T engineer* | McNealy-Bumberry Engineering, Inc., *structural engineer* | Claxton Consulting Engineers, *civil engineer* | Austin Tao & Associates, *landscape architect* | Brinkmann Construction, *General Contractor*
Project Awards & Recognition: John M. Clancy Award for Socially Responsible Housing, *Boston Society of Architects* | The Building of America Plaque of Honor, *Construction Communications* | Excellence in Masonry Award, Distinction in Design, *Masonry Institute of St. Louis* | Regional Excellence Award, *St. Louis Construction News & Review*
Photo Credits: Sam Fentress

US Custom House and Post Office
Collaborators: Trivers, *architect, interior design* | EDM, Inc., *MEP engineer* | KPFF Consulting Engineers, *structural engineer* | Kowelman Engineering, Inc., *civil engineering* | Lerch Bates Inc., *vertical transportation* | SWT Design, Inc. (Spaid Associates), *landscape architecture* | Randy Burketwhen did t Lighting Design, Inc., *lighting design* | BSI Contractors, *General Contractor*
Project Awards & Recognition: Government Design Award, *International Interior Design Association* | Merit Award for Architecture, *American Institute of Architects St. Louis* | Justice Facilities Review, *American Institute of Architects Academy of Architecture for Justice Knowledge Community* | John H. Poelker Levee Stone Award, *Downtown St. Louis Partnership*
Photo Credits: Bob Shimer/Hedrich Blessing, *pages 60, 63-67* | Sam Fentress, *page 62* | Library of Congress, Prints & Photographs Division, HABS no. MO-1195-1, Paul Piaget, photographer, *page 69*

Hipolito F. Garcia Federal Building and US Courthouse
Collaborators: Trivers, *architect, interior design* | Ford Powell & Carson, Inc., *associate architect* | IMEG (TTG Goetting), *MEP engineer* | ABSG Consulting, *structural engineer* | Construction Cost Systems, *cost estimating* | Lerch Bates, Inc., *vertical transportation* | Randy Burkett Lighting Design, Inc., *lighting design* | Rolf Jensen & Associates, Inc, *fire protection* | William Tao & Associates, *sustainability design and LEED consultation* | Jim Whitten Roofing Consultants, Inc., *envelope consultant* | Beck Contracting, *General Contractor*
Project Awards & Recognition: Excellence in Design Award – Institutional/Government, Renovation, *Environmental Design + Construction* | 5th Annual Green Building Awards, Bill Sinkin Solar Technology Award, *City of San Antonio* |

5th Annual Green Building Awards, Commercial Construction – Publicly Funded Award, *City of San Antonio* | Best Sustainable Project, *San Antonio Downtown Alliance* | Energy Star National Building Competition – Largest One-Year Energy Drop of any Office | Building in the National Energy Star Portfolio, *National Energy Star*
Photo Credits: Mark Menjivar

Gateway Arch National Park MSA
Photo Credits: Courtesy of Gateway Arch Park Foundation, *pages 78-81* | Cooper Robertson, *page 82*

Gateway Arch National Park – Ranger Station
Collaborators: Trivers, *architect, interior design* | KAI Design & Build, *MEP/FP engineer* | KPFF Consulting Engineers, *structural engineer* | David Mason & Associates, Inc., *civil engineer* | DG2 Design, *landscape architect* | Cohen Hilberry, *accessibility consultant* | IMEG, *technology engineer* | Everest Estimating LLC, *cost estimating* | SCI Engineering, *geotechnical engineer* | RB Construction Company, *General Contractor*
Photo Credits: Sam Fentress

Gateway Arch National Park – Arch Museum
Collaborators: Cooper Robertson, *architect of record* | James Carpenter Design Associates, *associate architect* | Trivers, *associate architect* | Michael Van Valkenburgh Associates, *landscape architect* | Haley Sharpe Design, *exhibit designer* | Alper Audi, *structural engineer* | Eckersley O'Callaghan, *structural glazing/façade* | Cowell Engineering, *exhibit structural design* | IMEG Corp., *ME/T engineer* | KAI Design & Build, *plumbing & fire protection engineer* | Tillotson Design Associates, *lighting designer* | Jaffe Holden, *av consultant* | Shen Milsom Wilke, *telecom/electronic security* | Van Deusen & Associates, *vertical transportation* | Henshell & Buccellato, *waterproofing consultant* | Hellmuth Bicknese, *LEED consultant* | Acousticontrol, *acoustical* | Cohen Hilberry Architects, *accessibility/universal design consultant* | Randy Burkett Lighting Design, *lighting designer* | Landtech Design, *irrigation designer* | Hydro Dramatics, *fountain designer* | Olsson Associates, *soil scientist* | Ecological Landscape Management, *ecological arborist* | David Mason & Associates, *roadway civil /structural engineer* | Civil Design, Inc., *stormwater civil design* | Geotechnology, *geotechnical engineer* | McCarthy Building Companies, *General Contractor*
Project Awards & Recognition:
Merit Award, Architecture, *American Institute of Architects Central States* | Honor Award, Craftsmanship, *American Institute of Architects St. Louis* | The American Architecture Award, The Chicago Athenaeum: *Museum of Architecture + Design and the European Centre for Architecture Art Design + Urban Studies* | Modernism in America Award of Excellence, Civic, *DOCOMOMO* | Design Award of Excellence, *Society of American Registered Architects* | Reconstruction Awards, Gold Award Winner, *Building Design + Construction* | Award of Excellence, *American Council of Engineering Companies* | Grand Award, *American Council of Engineering Companies Missouri* | Project of the Year, Building St. Louis Awards, *St. Louis Business Journal* | Award of Excellence, *International Association of Lighting Designers* | Award of Distinction, *Illuminating Engineering Society* | Global Best Project, Cultural, *Engineering News Record* | Outstanding Achievement, Whole Building, *AL Light + Architecture* | Honor Award, Architecture, *American Institute of Architects St. Louis* | Best of Year, Large Museum/Gallery Category, *Interior Design Magazine* | Best Architecture of 2018: Building for Complex Experiences, *Wall Street Journal* | Eight Best Buildings Completed in 2018, *Architectural Digest*
Photo Credits: ©Nic Lehoux, *pages 89-93* | Charlie Mayer, *page 91*

Gateway Arch National Park – Kiener Plaza Visitor Services Center
Collaborators: Trivers, *architect* | IMEG Corp., *MEP/T engineer* | KPFF Consulting Engineers, *structural engineer* | Civil Design, Inc., *civil engineer* | General Contractor: Hof Construction
Project Awards & Recognition: Distinguished Award, Small Projects, *American Institute of Architects St. Louis*
Photo Credits: Sam Fentress

Gateway Arch National Park – Old Courthouse
Collaborators: Trivers, *architect, interior design* | IMEG Corp., *MEP/T engineer* | KPFF Consulting Engineers, *structural engineer* | Civil Design, Inc., *civil engineer* | SWT Design, *landscape architect* | Kuhlmann Leavitt, Inc., *signage/wayfinding* | Cohen Hilberry, *accessibility* | Crawford Consulting Inc, *cost estimating* | Code Consultants Inc., *code* | Geotechology, *site investigation* | Professional Environmental Engineers, *environmental* | ATIS,

Credits

elevator consultant | Haley Sharpe Design, *exhibit designer* | General Contractor: Tarlton
Project Awards & Recognition: Most Enhanced Award, *Landmarks Association of St. Louis*
Photo Credits: Sam Fentress

I. Jerome and Rosemary Flance Early Childhood Education Center

Collaborators: Trivers, *architect, interior design* | SSC Engineering, Inc., *MEP/structural engineer* | Civil Design, Inc., *civil engineer* | Design Extra, *FFE* | SWT Design, Inc., *landscape architecture* | Code Consultants Inc., *code consultant* | Brinkmann Simms Construction, *General Contractor*
Project Awards & Recognition: AIA/HUD Secretary's Award: Community-Informed Design Award, *American Institute of Architects, US Department of Housing and Urban Development* | Merit Award, Architecture, *American Institute of Architects St. Louis*
Photo Credits: Alise O'Brien

Adam Aronson Fine Arts Center

Collaborators: Trivers, *architect, interior design* | KJWW Engineering Consultant (IMEG), *MEP/FP engineer* | Alper Audi, Inc., *structural engineer* | Farnsworth Group, Inc, *civil engineer* | SWT Design, Inc., *landscape architect* | Envision Lighting Design, LLC, *lighting design* | Cooper Construction Estimating, *cost estimating* | BSI Contractors, *General Contractor*
Project Awards & Recognition: Honor Award, Excellence in Architecture, *American Institute of Architects Central States* | Merit Award, Architecture, *American Institute of Architects St. Louis* | Distinguished Award, Unbuilt, *American Institute of Architects St. Louis*
Photo Credits: Sam Fentress

University of Pikeville Health Professions Education Building

Collaborators: Trivers, *architect,* | Ayers Saint Gross, *associate architect, interior design* | IMEG, *MEP/FP engineer* | Brown + Kubican Structural Engineers, *structural engineer* | Summit Engineering, Inc., *civil engineer* | Code Consultants, Inc., *code consultant* | The Sextant Group, *technology* | Codell Construction Company, *General Contractor*
Project Awards & Recognition: Merit Award, Architecture, *American Institute of Architects St. Louis* | Merit Award, New Construction Greater than $15M, *American Institute of Architects Kentucky* | Optometry School of the Year, *National Optometric Association*
Photo Credits: Sam Fentress

Woodward Lofts

Collaborators: Trivers, *architect, interior design* | G&W Engineering Corp., *MEP engineer* | KPFF Consulting Engineers, *structural engineer* | Civil Design, Inc., *civil engineer* | Designed Acoustics, *acoustic engineer* | Designery, *interior/exterior signage* | ARCO Construction, *General Contractor*
Project Awards & Recognition: Housing Award, *American Institute of Architects* | Palladio Awards, *Traditional Building* | Metamorphosis Award, Honorable Mention, Multifamily, *Retrofit Magazine* | Preserve Missouri Award, *Missouri Preservation* | Honor Award, *Architecture, American Institute of Architects St. Louis* | Most Enhanced Award, *Landmarks Association of St. Louis*
Photo Credits: Sam Fentress | Missouri Historical Society Archives, *page 148*

Tower Grove Park Pavilions

Collaborators: Trivers, *architect* | Custom Engineering, Inc., *EP engineer* | KPFF Consulting Engineers, *structural engineer* | Civil Design, Inc., *civil engineer* | Randy Burkett Lighting Design, *lighting design* | Vanstar Construction Co., *General Contractor*
Project Awards & Recognition: Palladio Award, *Traditional Building* | Most Enhanced Award, *Landmarks Association of St. Louis* | Honor Award, Craftsmanship, *American Institute of Architects St. Louis*
Photo Credits: Sam Fentress, *pages 154, 157-168, 161* | Courtesy of the Historic American Buildings Survey, National Park Service, US Department of the Interior. HABS no. MO-1137-I, *page 156* | Vanstar Construction, *pages 159,163 (aerial images)*

DOORWAYS

Collaborators: Trivers, *architect, interior design* | G&W Engineering Corp., *MEP engineer* | KPFF Consulting Engineers, *structural engineer* | Civil Design, Inc., *civil engineer* | Arbolope Studio, *landscape architect* | BSI Contractors, *General Contractor*
Photo Credits: Sam Fentress, pages 164-169 | ©Serhii Chrucky/Esto, *pages 170-171*

The Victor

Collaborators: Trivers, *architect, interior design* | IMEG, *MEP engineer* | KPFF Consulting Engineers, *structural engineer* | Reed Burkett Lighting Design, *lighting design* | Civil Design, Inc., *civil engineer* | Arbolope Studio, *landscape architect* | Cohen Hilberry, *accessibility consultant* | Wollenberg Building Conservation, LLC, *masonry consultant* | Paric Corporation, *General Contractor*
Project Awards & Recognition: Housing Award, *American Institute of Architects* | Distinguished Award in Preservation and Adaptive Reuse, *American Institute of Architects St. Louis* | Citation Award, Architecture, *American Institute of Architects Central States* | Preserve Missouri Award, *Missouri Preservation* | Most Enhanced Award, *Landmarks Association of St. Louis*
Photo Credits: Sam Fentress | Missouri Historical Society Archives, *page 183*

Additional Photography Credits:

Shaun Dodson (*cover*) | Sam Fentress (*The Victor, Trivers Office, Timeline; pages 11, 14, 188-193*) | ©Block, Inc *(The Post Building; page 8)* | Alise O'Brien *(Timeline; pages 188-191)* | Photos courtesy of McCormack Baron Salazar *(Timeline; pages 188-191)*

Contributors

Trivers

In 1975, Trivers was founded in St. Louis on values that still characterize the firm today: creating architecture of lasting positive consequence. In a city renowned for its historic architecture but in need of restoration and fresh ideas, we established a reputation for thoughtful design that responds to context. While our early work focused on historic renovation and adaptive reuse, we quickly expanded to include ground-up construction, balancing preservation with innovation.

Today, as an architecture, planning, urban design, and interiors firm, we remain committed to St. Louis while working with clients across the country. Our expertise spans civic, education, hospitality, housing, and workplace design—creating spaces that connect people, place, and purpose.

John Berglund

John Berglund, an architect turned developer, is the co-founder and managing partner of The StarWood Group, specializing in real estate and business acquisitions. He led the $75M redevelopment of the former Post Dispatch Building into Block's Midwest headquarters, establishing the "Downtown North Insite District" to attract geospatial and fintech companies to St. Louis. Additionally, he manages the McKelvey family office, supporting Jim McKelvey, co-founder and co-inventor of Square Mobile Payments.

Acknowledgments

To our clients and partners—thank you for your continued trust and the opportunities that have allowed us to pursue work with purpose and impact. Your support has shaped who we are and the legacy we continue to build.

To the talented individuals who have been part of the Trivers team—past and present—and to our founder, Andy Trivers: Your creativity, dedication, and passion for design have shaped our evolution and brought meaningful projects to life. This publication is as much a reflection of your contributions as it is of our shared vision.

Special thanks to our monograph team—Kara Brotherton, Carie Dunn, Charity Seyer, and Common Ground Public Relations—for leading the curation, design, writing, and editing of this book and for thoughtfully telling our story.

We extend our appreciation to John Berglund for his insightful foreword, to the team at ORO Editions for their guidance throughout this process, and to the talented photographers whose artistry and expertise beautifully capture the spirit of our work.

ORO Editions
Publishers of Architecture, Art, and Design
Gordon Goff: Publisher

www.oroeditions.com
info@oroeditions.com
Published by ORO Editions

Author: Trivers
Book Design: Charity Seyer, with Pablo Mandel/CircularStudio
Project Manager: Jake Anderson
10 9 8 7 6 5 4 3 2 1 First Edition
ISBN: 978-1-961856-92-9
Prepress and Print work by ORO Editions Inc.
Printed in China

ORO Editions makes a continuous effort to minimize the overall carbon footprint of its publications. As part of this goal, ORO, in association with Global ReLeaf, arranges to plant trees to replace those used in the manufacturing of the paper produced for its books. Global ReLeaf is an international campaign run by American Forests, one of the world's oldest nonprofit conservation organizations. Global ReLeaf is American Forests' education and action program that helps individuals, organizations, agencies, and corporations improve the local and global environment by planting and caring for trees.